# Data protection for library and information services

Paul Ticher

INFORMATION MANAGEMENT

# Is your organisation a corporate member of Aslib?

Aslib-IMI is a world class corporate membership organisation with over 2000 members in some 70 countries. Aslib actively promotes best practice in the management of information resources. It lobbies on all aspects of the management of, and legislation concerning, information at local, national and international levels.

Aslib provides consultancy and information services, professional development training, conferences, specialist recruitment, Internet products, and publishes primary and secondary journals, conference proceedings, directories and monographs.

Further information is available from:

Aslib-IMI
Staple Hall
Stone House Court
London EC3A 7PB
Tel: +44 (0) 20 7903 0000
Fax: +44 (0) 20 7903 0011
Email: *aslib@aslib.com*
WWW: *www.aslib.com*

# Series Editor

Sylvia Webb is a well-known consultant, author and lecturer in the information management field. Her first book, *Creating an Information Service*, now in its third edition, was published by Aslib and has sold in over forty countries. She has experience of working in both the public and private sectors, ranging from public libraries to national and international organisations. She has also been a lecturer at Ashridge Management College, specialising in management and interpersonal skills, which led to her second book, *Personal Development in Information Work*, also published by Aslib. She has served on a number of government advisory bodies and is past Chair of the former Information and Library Services Lead Body, now the Information Services National Training Organisation which develops National and Scottish Vocational Qualifications (NVQs and SVQs) for the LIS profession. She is actively involved in professional education and training and is also a former Vice-President of the Institute of Information Scientists. As well as being editor of this series, Sylvia Webb has written three of the Know How Guides: *Making a charge for library and information services*, *Preparing a guide to your library and information service* and *Knowledge management: linchpin of change*.

A complete listing of all titles in the series can be found at the back of this volume.

# About the author

Paul Ticher is an independent information systems consultant, specialising in information management, IT and Data Protection. After working in a variety of campaigns and voluntary organisations, he spent five years at the Community Information Project, providing support on IT issues to library-based community information services and to voluntary and statutory advice agencies. Here he researched and wrote *At the touch of a button*, a pioneering survey of the role of IT in providing better public access to information.

At this time he also became involved with the implementation of the 1984 Data Protection Act. He wrote extensively on its implications, delivered highly popular briefing sessions, and developed guidelines on Data Protection for several different types of service.

Paul was briefly Chief Officer of a small national charity, then became an independent consultant in 1991. He has maintained his interest in Data Protection, and followed closely the evolution of the 1995 European Directive and the parliamentary progress of the 1998 Act. Paul is the author of *Data Protection for Voluntary Organisations* and co-author of *Information Management for Voluntary and Community Organisations* (both published by Directory of Social Change, 2000). He has written numerous articles on IT and Data Protection, has delivered training on Data Protection the length and breadth of the country and has acted as consultant to organisations large and small. He can be contacted at paul@paulticher.com.

# Disclaimer

Whilst the author of this book has tried to ensure the accuracy of this publication, the publishers and the author cannot accept any liability for errors, omissions, or mistakes.

All of the URL's listed in this book were checked during June 2001 and were working at that time.

# Contents

# Introduction

At first sight, Data Protection may not appear to affect the library professional unduly. The 1998 Data Protection Act only applies to information about people. Most of the material held in a typical library will not be covered.

But this first impression would be wrong. Librarians deal with people every day. They hold information about these people, and have a responsibility to handle the information properly. Librarians may also be called on to advise their colleagues on matters relating to information-handling. Data Protection could clearly come under this heading.

And librarians are clearly Data Subjects in their own right, so have an interest in knowing that their own data, and that of their colleagues, is being treated in the appropriate way.

Data Protection is about treating people fairly. 'Fair' use of data has been described as comprising the following four elements:

- Notice – in other words, do people know what is going on with their data?
- Choice – wherever possible, over the way their data is used.
- Security – a guarantee that their data is being properly looked after.

1

- Access – the opportunity to check and correct if necessary the data that is being held
  about them.

The Act lays down a solid framework for fair use
of data, mainly through the eight Data Protection
Principles. However, the Act cannot stand alone.
It clearly interacts with an organisation's policies
on confidentiality and security, as well as other
policies regarding the data held on employees, service users, and the like.

It is worth bearing in mind two general points
throughout. The Act very rarely *prevents* you from
doing anything reasonable. What it does, though,
is ask you to do it in the right way, and with regard
to the interests of the Data Subject. Also, it very
rarely takes precedence over other legislation. If
another law requires you to do something, you can
be fairly certain that the Data Protection Act will
not stand in your way (or be available as an excuse
not to).

There is no 'standard' way of applying Data Protection. Although the same rules apply to everyone, they have to be interpreted in the particular
circumstances of each organisation. This means that
a lot must be left to the judgement of the people in
each organisation in drawing up appropriate policies and procedures. Data Protection is not just a
matter of applying a few simple rules. Rather, it is
a matter of applying *principles* whose implications
have to be thought through.

This book is designed to explain the principles un-
derlying Data Protection, and to help the reader
think through how best to apply them in the li-

brary situation. It cannot be a full statement of the law. The reader is advised to take qualified professional legal advice if they face a situation which takes them outside the scope of this book or where they feel that they have a problem which requires specific guidance.

In this book 'the Act' means the UK 1998 Data Protection Act, unless the context requires otherwise, but many other countries take an interest in this area and will have official contacts accordingly (see p. 105).

# Brief definitions

These are brief explanatory definitions. **Bold** text indicates that the full definition of the term in the Act is given in Appendix 5.

**Data:** information held on or intended to be held on an automated system (including computers) or a **relevant filing system**, or held by public authorities.

**Data Controller:** the legal 'person' who decides and takes responsibility for why (the 'purpose for which') and how (the 'manner in which') personal data is **processed**. Almost always the employer is the Data Controller, not individual employees.

**Data Processor:** an organisation (or individual) that **processes personal data** on behalf of a **Data Controller.**

**Data Subject:** the person about whom **personal data** is held.

3

European Economic Area (EEA): the members of the European Union — Austria, Belgium, Denmark, Finland, France, Germany, Greece, Ireland, Italy, Luxembourg, the Netherlands, Portugal, Spain, Sweden and the UK — plus Iceland, Liechtenstein and Norway.

Information Commissioner: the public official responsible to the UK Parliament for administering and enforcing the Data Protection Act (and other matters, including Freedom of Information). Previously known as the Data Protection Commissioner and, before that, the Data Protection Registrar.

**Personal data: data** relating to an identifiable, living individual.

**Processing:** anything you do with **personal data** from obtaining it, using it, holding it and disclosing it, all the way through to disposing of it.

**Relevant filing system:** a set of manual information, structured so that specific information relating to a particular individual can be readily found.

**Sensitive personal data: personal data** relating to the **Data Subject**'s race or ethnic background, religion, politics, Trade Union membership, health, sex life or criminal record.

# 1. Personal data

The Act applies to 'personal data'. Both elements in the phrase are important. The 'personal' part relates to information about an *identifiable, living individual*. This means that the person must be identifiable by the organisation that holds the data. Normally, you should assume that a name and some other detail is enough to make someone identifiable.

Because the Act applies to information about *individuals*, it does not affect the information you may hold about *organisations*. However, Data Protection does apply to contact details of people within those organisations.

As well as being 'personal', the information must be 'data'. This means that it must fall into one of the following categories:

- It is held on a computer or other automated system.
- It is held in a 'relevant filing system'. This means a set of information *structured* so that specific information relating to a particular individual can be readily located. Many card indexes and paper filing systems are likely to be included.
- It is intended to form part of one of the above computer or manual systems. Forms on which

data is collected, or even the notes from a telephone conversation, would be covered, for example.

- It forms part of an 'accessible' record held by a public authority. These are records to which subject access was previously available through separate legislation, and include health, education and social work records.

- It is held by a public authority, even if it does not fall into any of the categories above. (This relates to material covered by the Freedom of Information Act 2000. Note that this book does not deal with issues that arise specifically in relation to this Act.)

Data can be any information which can be related to the individual, not just text. It could therefore include photographs, audio and video material, records from automatic systems such as CCTV or a swipe-card security system, medical data. The test is whether the data relates to identifiable, living individuals *and* is held on computer, in a relevant manual filing system, etc.

Under the 1998 Act the definition of data is far wider than it used to be under the old (1984) Act, which only applied to certain records held on computer, and not to manual files at all. This means that much more information is now within the scope of Data Protection, and it affects far more people and activities.

# Examples

- The borrowers on my loans system are identifiable on the computer only by the bar code on their ticket. However, there is a separate record of which ticket has been issued to whom. The main computer record is clearly personal data, because the people can be identified from the supplementary files.

- Visitors to our building have to sign in. The paper signing in book is not personal data, because it is not structured so that I can easily look up information about a particular person (such as the times they came and went, or the number of their car).

- The details of authors in a library catalogue system may be personal data; but since this information is already in the public domain you are unlikely to have to take specific Data Protection action over any obvious and reasonable use of the information.

- The names, job titles, e-mail addresses and direct phone numbers of the people on our contact database are likely to be personal data. The information about the company or organisation they work for is not.

# 2. The eight Data Protection Principles

Anything you do with personal data must comply with the Data Protection Principles. These are at the heart of the Data Protection Act.

In summary, the eight principles say:

- Personal data must be processed fairly and lawfully. The Act elaborates on the measures required for fairness.

- You must obtain personal data only for a specified purpose or purposes and use it only in ways that are compatible with the original purpose(s).

- Personal data must be adequate, relevant and not excessive.

- Personal data must be accurate and, where necessary, kept up to date.

- Personal data must not be held longer than necessary.

- You must respect the rights of Data Subjects.

- You must have appropriate security.

- Transferring personal data abroad is subject to additional rules.

For the full text of the Principles, see Appendix 1.

# 'Processing'

The Principles refer to 'processing' personal data. The definition of processing in the Act is very broad, including: obtaining the data, holding or storing it, using it in any way, changing it, passing it on to others, erasing it or destroying it. This means that from the moment you acquire the data, right up to the time you dispose of it, you have to treat it properly.

# Purposes

Many of the principles refer to your 'purpose(s)' in holding the data. Where Data Protection is concerned the 'purposes' defined by the Information Commissioner are fairly general. Everything to do with personnel, for example — including pay, pensions, holiday and sickness records, work planning and so on — would be within the 'Staff Administration' purpose. Much library work would come under 'Information and databank administration'. See also the Chapter on **Notification**, page 88.

# 3. Who is responsible for data protection?

## The Data Controller

The Act gives the main responsibility for Data Protection to the 'Data Controller'. This is the 'person' who decides why and how personal data is processed. However, a 'person' does not have to be an individual; a company (or any 'incorporated' organisation) is also a legal person. Although an individual can be a Data Controller in their own right, it is much more likely that the organisation you work for will be the Data Controller.

This is reassuring for anyone who is carrying out activities on behalf of their employer. Even if a specific employee is made responsible for Data Protection compliance, the organisation itself remains the Data Controller. You are only likely to be personally liable if you 'knowingly or recklessly' contravene your employer's policies and procedures. (See also the chapter on **Enforcement and penalties**, page 95.)

An organisation cannot be a Data Controller on behalf of another organisation. This means that each separate legal entity has to consider whether it is a Data Controller, even if they are all part of a group, trading to the outside world as a single body. The group may well lay down common standards, but it will not be the Data Controller for data held or used by individual companies.

Where organisations work together, they may be Data Controllers jointly over the same data. This can be a complex situation. Each Data Controller should operate to the same standards, and has to be able to trust the other(s) to handle data responsibly — or bear a share of the responsibility if things go wrong. It is likely to be worth agreeing in writing how this relationship will be handled, and to take legal advice if in any doubt.

## The Data Protection Compliance Officer

Data Protection must be given some consideration at Board or senior management level, who need to satisfy themselves that the organisation has put the necessary measures in place. Day to day responsibility for compliance should then be allocated to the appropriate member of staff or department.

Options include:

- The legal department. This has the benefit of putting Data Protection on the same footing as a range of other legal matters, but may be somewhat remote from day to day operations.

- Internal audit or quality standards. The advantage of putting Data Protection here is that the *activities* involved with Data Protection are likely to overlap with other areas of concern.

- Information services. Because there are substantial elements of information management in Data Protection, it may be appropriate to use people with these specific skills as a central resource for the organisation.

- **Public relations.** Good Data Protection practice can enhance an organisation's image and help to build trust with those outside.

- Customer service. **Most Data Protection** issues are likely to arise between the organisation and customers or service users who are either unhappy or suspicious already.

- Human resources. If an organisation has relatively little contact with individuals outside, most of the Data Protection questions that arise may be to do with staff records.

- Information technology. In the past it was common to make the IT Manager responsible for Data Protection, because it only applied to data held on computer. Now that Data Protection extends to manual records as well, this is less appropriate. IT staff do still need to be involved, however.

What it comes down to is that the Data Protection Compliance Officer, wherever they are located, will have to work closely with people from all over the organisation to ensure that policies and procedures are consistent and comprehensive. Even if the library or information services department has excellent Data Protection practice, the organisation as a whole will remain vulnerable unless all departments take it equally seriously.

The Compliance Officer will also have to ensure that all staff are given the guidance, information and support they need so that when they handle personal data in the course of their work they are enabled to comply with the organisation's policies and procedures. (See also the chapter on the **Data Protection Compliance Officer**, page 100.)

# Other staff

Although ultimate responsibility lies with the Data Controller, through the Compliance Officer, Data Protection is not just a matter of setting down a policy and forgetting about it. What matters is what happens day by day in relation to real people and real data. It is therefore important that all staff who handle personal data understand the basic principles and their organisation's policies and procedures. Data Protection awareness must permeate the whole organisation.

# The Data Processor

Many routine activities nowadays are outsourced. Where these involve the processing of personal data, the company that actually carries out the work will usually be a Data Processor. For example, a Data Controller might use external agencies to provide a payroll service, mailing facilities, marketing, delivery of mail-order goods, IT support and many other services.

In these cases the essential distinction is that the Data Processor has no interest in the content of the data they are processing. They don't decide who will be paid or how much; they just do the sums and get the bank transfers to the right place at the right time. They don't decide which information will be mailed to which person (although as a marketing company they may give advice on this). They are not concerned with the content of the database they are recovering from a crashed disk.

In this situation the Data Controller retains all the Data Protection responsibility. In order to underline this, the Act specifies that there must be a written contract between the Data Controller and the Data Processor, making it clear that the Processor is just following the Data Controller's instructions. In addition, the Data Processor must be able to show that they have appropriate security and the Data Controller has a specific responsibility to be satisfied that the security is adequate.

You may well need to take legal advice to ensure that suitable contracts are in place.

# 4. Informing the data subject

One of the central tenets of the Act, and one that should make a considerable difference once it is universally applied, is that it is essentially unfair to do things behinds people's backs. In most cases, 'fair' processing requires that the Data Subject should know who is processing data about them, and for what purpose.

This does not always mean that you need to go out of your way to slap a Data Protection statement on every form and document. In many cases it will be entirely obvious who is collecting or using data and what for. If the main users of your information service are internal, then any information you hold about them is likely to be ancillary to that held by the organisation as a matter of course on all its employees. You would rarely need to explain anything further.

Even if your users are external, whether it is members of the public borrowing books from a lending library, members of an association phoning the association's information service, or customers ordering information products, they may already be perfectly aware of what is happening with their data from the context in which they provide it.

Where you do need to provide additional information is if any user of the data or any use to which the data will be put is not obvious. Examples might include:

- If the details of people who call your enquiry line are automatically shared with the marketing department.

- If people who attend a conference or training course will be added to your database and invited to future events.

- If it is not clear who the Data Controller is because your service is provided from someone else's premises.

- If details of people who use your service are passed to your sponsor or funding body for audit purposes or for them to contact the users directly. (Passing anonymous data or statistics doesn't involve personal data, of course, and is therefore outside the Act.)

You should always try to put yourself in the position of a relatively uninformed Data Subject. Things that might be 'obvious' to you, with your inside knowledge, may not be so obvious to the ordinary user.

You need to be particularly careful if the information is intended to be widely disclosed — for example in a printed directory for sale or distribution, in response to enquiries from the public, or on a web site. It is very important that before people part with their information they should know as much as possible about the circumstances in which it will be disclosed, how much control you exercise over the people who have access to it, and whether they are able to specify any conditions or restrictions around the disclosure.

Finally, people should know how to take things further if they want to. How can they exercise their rights of subject access or opting out of direct marketing? (See the chapters on **People's right to see their own records**, page 47 and **Restrictions on direct marketing**, page 56.) Who should they contact if they want more information?

The only time you are allowed to process personal data without the Data Subject knowing for certain what is going on is if:

- you obtained the data from a third party (not the Data Subject themselves), *and*

- informing the Data Subject would involve you in 'disproportionate effort'.

Examples of where this might apply could include the names of people within organisations on your contact database. Clearly they would not be surprised to find themselves there for business purposes, and you are not expected to phone them up and say 'by the way, welcome to our contact database'. The same provision might also apply to information that is already in the public domain, which you are using for obvious and reasonable purposes.

If you rely on the 'disproportionate effort' provision, you must keep a record of your reasons for believing that it applies.

# Other requirements for 'fair' processing

Providing just the information set out above is not necessarily enough, on its own, to guarantee fair processing. You must also give the Data Subject any other information that is needed to make your processing fair. This deliberately vague provision means that you must put yourself in the position of the Data Subject and consider whether there is anything else they should know — for example, are you able to give them any assurances about security or confidentiality which will help them decide whether to entrust their data to you? Or, by contrast, is there any particular security risk that they should be aware of?

It is automatically unfair to deceive or mislead anyone when you obtain personal data. If you agree to exchange your mailing list with another organisation, both sides must be honest about how they are going to use the names and addresses. If you offer people the chance to participate in a 'user feedback' survey, this must not be a disguised marketing exercise.

You must also, according to the first Data Protection Principle, meet at least one of the 'fair processing conditions' that are set out in Schedule 2 of the Act (see Appendix 2). Because this raises the question of Data Subject consent for the use you make of their data, this is covered separately in the following chapter.

# How to provide the information

As long as the Data Subject knows what they need to know, it doesn't matter how they get the information. Some of the possibilities might include:

- You include a Data Protection statement on your data collection forms or in your telephone script.

- You put a short article or statement in a newsletter or bulletin, telling everyone who receives it what they need to know.

- You issue a welcome letter to every new Data Subject, which includes the relevant information.

- You have a prominent notice where your Data Subjects will see it.

- Information is included in a staff handbook or induction material for new staff.

- You produce an information sheet which is available on request and prominently advertised.

- They know it already, or it is obvious from the context or from the history of their relationship with you. (But are you really confident that this is the case?)

- After due consideration, where the data has been received from a third party, you decide that providing the information would involve disproportionate effort.

# Examples

- My organisation carries out CCTV monitoring of public areas of the building. On consulting the Information Commissioner's Code of Practice on the use of CCTV we realise that we need to put up prominent notices advising people that they are being monitored.

- I hold a reference book that lists lawyers and their areas of expertise, which I use in order to advise people who need a lawyer. The book is probably personal data, but no one who is in it would expect to be contacted by everyone who buys it and uses it for its intended purpose. However, when I transfer the information from the book to my own database so that I can try to sell the lawyers a subscription to our information service, I decide that I should provide them with full information about the Data Controller and Purposes the first time I contact them, and make it clear how they can be taken off the database.

- I decide to produce a directory of specialists working in the field that my company is interested in. I compile it from public sources, principally journals and the like. While this is only used internally, I can probably argue that it would involve 'disproportionate effort' to inform the Data Subjects. However, I then decide that it is so useful I will smarten it up and produce a version for sale to our customers. At this point it is clear that I should tell them what is going on — and incidentally improve the final product by giving them the chance to correct, update and add to the information that I hold.

- My department has a training suite as well as an information service. The training is provided by a range of external agencies, although we handle the bookings. I decide that it is not obvious to the Data Subjects that the eventual Data Controller may be one of a number of training agencies, so I revise our booking form to include this information.

- Our university library is required to collaborate with other authorities in tracking down students who are in debt. Because this Purpose is not obvious to the students when they sign up as borrowers, we decide to put a statement in the guidance provided to all new borrowers.

- I have been asked to undertake a competitor intelligence exercise, building up profiles of key people in competitor firms without their knowledge. The information will obviously come from third parties, so can I use the 'disproportionate effort' argument to avoid blowing the whole thing by telling the Data Subjects what we are doing? With some hesitation I decide that information in the public domain — such as papers the Data Subjects have published, or factual media reports — is probably not a problem. However, as soon as we start adding information given to us privately, there is a strong case that the Data Subjects could claim a right to know what is going on. I suggest that we should take legal advice before proceeding.

# 5. When do you need consent?

There is a prevalent myth that under the new Act you always need the permission of the Data Subject if you want to use their personal data. This is untrue. However, the Act certainly encourages the Data Controller to seek consent, and in certain cases does require it.

The issue of consent must be separated from the provision of information. The requirement to provide information to the Data Subject exists regardless of whether consent is being sought or not. In practice, however, where you are seeking consent it is quite likely that this will be done at the same time as you provide information.

The Data Subject's consent is one of the 'conditions' for fair processing set out in Schedule 2 of the Act (see Appendix 2). Any processing is unfair if it does not meet *at least one* of the six conditions which are, in brief:

- Processing with the consent of the Data Subject.
- Processing necessary in connection with a contract involving the Data Subject.
- Processing that you are obliged by law to undertake.
- Processing necessary to protect the 'vital interests' of the Data Subject.

- Processing in connection with judicial, government or public functions.

- Processing that is in your 'legitimate interests', provided that the Data Subject's rights, freedoms or legitimate interests are not infringed.

Remember that 'processing' covers anything you do with the data, including obtaining, holding it, using it, disclosing to others or disposing of it.

Provided your processing all meets at least one of the conditions, you can 'mix and match', relying on whichever is appropriate at any particular time. You may, for example, have a database where some people have given consent but others are there in your legitimate interests, without their consent. Or you may hold personnel data in connection with your employment contract but release it to various government agencies because of a legal obligation.

It is good practice to seek consent wherever possible. However, the Data Subject must have a genuine choice. There is a strong argument that it would be 'unfair' to ask for consent but then, if it is refused, to continue to process data under one of the other conditions.

Consent is not defined in the Act, but is covered in the European Directive on which the Act is based (95/46 EC). This states that consent must be 'specific, informed and freely given' and that the Data Subject must 'signify' their agreement. Consent can therefore probably be implied from an action taken by the Data Subject — if someone fills in an application form, in the knowledge of how the data will be used, they have probably consented to any use of the data which is obvious or which is specified on the form. However, it is less likely that you would have consent if you tell the Data Subject that you will do something unless they respond. Many commentators believe that if they fail to respond, they haven't 'signified' their consent.

There is no requirement for consent to be given in writing, but if you feel that evidence could be required in future some form of written record may be advisable.

Although consent must be 'freely given', you are allowed to point out the consequences of the Data Subject withholding their consent: 'If you don't allow us to keep your personal details in our record of your enquiry, we will not be able to alert you of future developments in the area you are interested in.'

# Processing without consent

Processing that is *necessary* in connection with a contract involving the Data Subject, and processing that is *necessary* in order to comply with a legal requirement (the second and third Conditions) do not need the Data Subject's consent. Most personnel records, for example, could well be processed under one or other of these conditions, as would the customer records of most paid-for services. It is important, however, to pay attention to the requirement that the processing is *necessary*. The employer may, for example, want to process personnel records in a particular way; but if they *could* fulfil their part of the contract without that activity then consent may be required after all.

The Information Commissioner has suggested that processing without consent but in the Data Subject's 'vital interests' (the fourth Condition) should be reserved for emergencies only, rather than used routinely, and then only for genuine life and death situations. This guidance is considered by some to be over-restrictive; nonetheless it is clearly advisable to seek alternatives wherever possible.

For many official functions consent is not required because of the fifth Condition. This covers processing which is *necessary* for the administration of justice, for government functions, and for other functions 'of a public nature exercised in the public interest by any person'. If you are running a service as part of a public authority, or which you believe may fall under this definition, you should consult your legal department to find out whether your activities meet the fifth Condition.

Many information services will wish to process data, without seeking consent, under the sixth Condition — where processing is in your 'legitimate interests' and doesn't harm the Data Subject. This would be particularly relevant to records such as:

- Non-controversial information that is in the public domain, such as information about authors in a catalogue, or profiles of public figures in a reference book or database. You still have to be 'fair', however, as well as not infringing the 'rights, freedoms or legitimate interests' of the Data Subject, so any secret compiling of information to be used against people, even if it were publicly available, would probably not be allowable. (See, however, the limited exemption for literature, art and journalism in the chapter on **Exemptions**, page 83).

- Business contacts, where the information is genuinely used for business-to-business purposes. A good test here is probably 'if this person changed jobs, would I replace their name with the new post-holder's?' If instead you are interested in the specific individual you may need to consider the situation further.

- Records of people connected with your primary Data Subjects. For example, if you provide information or other services to individuals you may have a record of their solicitor, doctor or other professional, but you would not think of seeking consent from these people. Next of kin or emergency contact information, about staff, for instance, is less clear-cut. There may well be a case for at least informing the Data Subject that you hold their details and possibly for seeking consent.

In many of these cases you might have received the information from a Third Party. You could therefore decide that you do not need to inform the Data Subject that you are processing their data. The result is that in such cases your existing practice may well comply with the Act without you taking any specific action. Rather than just assume this, however, it would be wise to review the situation and record your conclusions, together with any limits beyond which information would need to be provided or consent sought.

## Examples

* Subscribers to our information service pay an annual fee. Many of them are professional private individuals, so the data that we hold about their financial transactions with us and their contact details is personal data. However, the arrangement with them is contractual and holding this information is necessary for the contract to be fulfilled. Therefore there is no need to seek consent.

* Our current awareness service is available to all employees of our organisation, but they have to ask for it and tell us how they want it delivered — by e-mail or on paper. Because they must take the initiative to provide us with the information, we can assume that they have consented to us holding it for that purpose.

* I have a database of local journalists, politicians and business leaders, which I use mainly for PR purposes. Because this use is in the 'legitimate interests' of the Data Controller and I judge that the rights, freedoms and legitimate interests of the Data Subjects are not being harmed, I decide that I do not need to seek consent. (As a matter of courtesy, if nothing else, I would take people off the database if they asked me to.)

- I organise conferences. In the past, as a matter of course I have been including the names and contact details of all delegates on a list that goes into the delegate pack. Under the new Act, however, I realise that this is not 'necessary' as part of the contract — unlike the invoicing and room allocations, for example. Is it, then, in my 'legitimate interests'. It may be, but I start to wonder if it might infringe the legitimate interests of the Data Subjects. They may have good reasons for not wanting their contact details publicised. At the same time, I realise that this use of the data may not be obvious. At some conferences, after all, delegates are not provided with each other's details. I therefore decide that I need to make it clear on the booking form that I would like to provide a full delegate list, but give people the options of being excluded, or listed only by name, without the contact details.

# 6. Processing 'sensitive' personal data

Special care must be taken where you are processing data defined in the Act as 'sensitive'. Briefly, this covers information about the Data Subject's:

- racial or ethnic origin;
- political opinions;
- religious beliefs or other beliefs of a similar nature;
- trade union membership;
- physical or mental health or condition;
- sexual life;
- commission or alleged commission of any offence;
- court proceedings.

Note that other information which the Data Subject may feel sensitive about — such as their age or financial information — is not caught by the definition.

If you process any sensitive personal data, you must comply with further conditions (set out in Schedule 3 of the Act, see Appendix 3) as well as the 'fair processing' conditions discussed in the previous chapter. There are a considerable number of these conditions, and those set out in the Act have been added to by Regulation (see Appendix 3 and **References and further reading**, page 102). However,

they are much more restrictive than the fair processing conditions, and in many cases the only one you
will be able to meet is the first Condition: the 'explicit' consent of the Data Subject.

'Explicit consent' is not defined in the Act, but guidance from the Information Commissioner indicates
that it requires the Data Subject to be given more
information about the uses to which their data will
be put, and that unlike straightforward 'consent'
it cannot be implied but must be actively indicated
— by a signature or a definite verbal assent.

Three other conditions for processing sensitive data
are perhaps worth looking at in the context of library and information services:

• The fifth condition allows you to process sensitive personal data without consent where
it has been deliberately made public by the
Data Subject. Where someone has stood as a
candidate for a political party, holds office in
a Trade Union, or has put themselves for-
ward as a spokesperson for a religious group,
for example, this means that you can, in effect, treat that particular data as though it
were not sensitive.

• The ninth condition, along with two conditions added by Regulation, allows you to
process some sensitive personal data for
equalities monitoring. The permitted data
covers the Data Subject's racial or ethnic origin, disability or religion. The processing must
only be for monitoring, with the aim of promoting equality. And in the case of disability
or religion, explicitly, you are not permitted

to use the information to make decisions about individuals (for example making special provision for a person with disabilities).

- Another condition added by Regulation provides that if you are offering a *confidential* service, such as counselling, advice or support, you may process sensitive data without consent in certain circumstances. You have to be able to show that your service is in the 'substantial public interest' and that seeking consent is either not possible or not reasonable, or would jeopardise the service.

The remainder of the conditions are likely to apply only in very particular circumstances, but if you do have sensitive data in any of your systems, or intend to, and there is any reason why you do not want or feel unable to seek consent, you should consult the complete list in Appendix 3.

You may also want to consider whether you actually need the sensitive data. Of course there will be circumstances where it is essential to your Purpose, but one aim of the Act is to get people to think carefully about their use of such data. If you can achieve what you want without holding sensitive data you both make your life easier and offer additional protection to the Data Subject.

## Examples

- I provide a confidential telephone information service about a particular medical condition. The people who phone me often give considerable amounts of sensitive personal data, which I record. Many of the people who phone are distressed, and on consideration I decide that it is reasonable not to seek consent. However, I do make it clear to every caller that the service is confidential, and that I am recording what they tell me, so that they have the option of asking for some of the information not to be kept.

- The booking form for our training courses asks if people have special needs, such as disabilities. Because this is sensitive, we decide that the form needs to spell out: that the information is being collected so that we can provide a better service but that giving it is optional; that it will be passed on to the trainer if that is relevant; and that we will only keep it until the specific course is completed. On that basis we ask for their consent to use the data. (An alternative might be to collect this information on a separate sheet which is not kept with the other data but in a file relating just to the course. In this case it may not be personal data, so that the requirement for consent would not apply. However, it would still be good practice to provide the information suggested above.)

# 7. Processing only for specific Purposes

The Second Data Protection Principle says that you must only obtain data for a specified Purpose or Purposes. This means that you must know what you are collecting or obtaining information for. You cannot accumulate personal data just in case it becomes useful.

Further, you need to think carefully if you subsequently spot an opportunity to use data for a Purpose it wasn't originally acquired for. The Act says that any use of the data must be 'compatible' with the original Purpose(s). If you decide to make use of the data for some new activity, it would be unwise to do this without ensuring that the Data Subjects know as soon as possible of the new Purpose. The further away from the original Purpose(s) this new activity is, the more important it is to ensure that the Data Subjects know what is going on, and that your processing is 'fair'. This may well require you to give them the opportunity to opt out of any secondary use of the data before you use it.

Analysis of personal data for statistics and its use for management of the service, quality control, etc. is always likely to be compatible with the Purpose it is held for. See also the special provisions for research, statistical and historical purposes in the chapter on **Exemptions**, page 83.

Disclosure to others is also 'processing'. The implication of the Second Principle is therefore that you cannot release personal data unless you are satisfied that the disclosure is 'compatible' with the Purpose(s) you hold it for (but see also the chapter on **Exemptions**, page 83.)

# Examples

* I record enquiries to my information service. One day, a colleague asks for the names of everyone who has recently asked about a particular topic, so that they can invite them to a free seminar on that subject by a visiting speaker. I never told my users that their data might be used in this way, but I decide on balance that the use is close enough to the original purpose to be 'compatible'.

* Our public library is about to offer an after-school homework club. The manager suggests that we should identify all the borrowers of school age from our central database and write to them about the club. After some discussion, however, we decide that some users may regard this as too far from the original Purpose to be compatible, so we settle on leaflets and posters in the library, and a presentation at local schools instead.

* My academic library holds the home addresses and phone numbers of people who borrow material so that I can chase up overdue material or ask if it could be returned early when someone else requests it. One day a tutor asks for the contact details of a stu-

dent, saying that they need to talk urgently about some overdue course work. Is this disclosure compatible with the Purpose I hold the information for? It is not always easy to tell. In this one-òff case I decide to consult colleagues before deciding what to do. If it happens often we will need to come up with a policy to handle such situations.

- We receive a grant to provide information to job-seekers in our area. When the time comes to put in our quarterly report, the funder asks that we give full details of all the clients we have worked with so that they can check that their money has been used appropriately. We argue that auditing our finances is not compatible with the Purpose we originally told the clients about — which was helping them to find work. We therefore ask the funder either to be satisfied with anonymous information about our users, or to rely on the procedures we have in place for recording and, eventually, auditing the use of the funds.

- In April 2001 a local councillor in the West Midlands was fined £500 plus £780 costs for Data Protection offences. During an election campaign he had used data about bus-pass holders, which he had legitimate access to as their local councillor, to target people for a party political mailing.

# 8. Monitoring employees and the public

Specific issues may arise where a Data Controller feels the need to monitor the behaviour of staff or members of the public. Obviously there are situations nowadays where this is regarded as routine. These include:

- Logging access to premises, whether by swipe cards or signing-in books.

- Closed-circuit television (CCTV) systems.

- Monitoring e-mails and other computer transactions.

While organisations usually have very good reasons for wanting to undertake monitoring, including protecting the physical security or staff and visitors, these situations do raise legitimate concerns, and it is no coincidence that among the first Codes of Practice issued by the Information Commissioner (see the chapter on **Codes of practice**, page 93) are ones covering the use of CCTV and the use of personal data on employees, which includes a section on monitoring.

Occasionally, monitoring systems may be found not to record personal data. For example a signing-in book, held entirely on paper, may not be a 'relevant filing system'. Where personal data is recorded, however, Data Protection considerations apply.

The first issue is therefore 'fair' processing, and this requires that the Data Subject should know who the Data Controller is and what they are collecting data for. This suggests that *covert* monitoring should be avoided. The Information Commissioner does give some examples where it might be permissible, but in general the Data Subject should be told what is happening. This may require, for example, placing notices in public areas that are subject to CCTV monitoring or including suitable information in a staff handbook.

The processing must then meet at least one of the Schedule 2 'Fair processing' conditions. Those likely to apply are probably only the First (consent) or Sixth (legitimate interests of the Data Controller). However, in the latter case the rights, freedoms and legitimate interests of the Data Subject must not be infringed. Bearing in mind the heightened awareness brought about by the UK Human Rights Act (1998) and equivalent legislation elsewhere, there could be contention over the extent to which monitoring without consent can be justified. The Data Controller's action must certainly be proportionate to the risk, and should only be undertaken if it is not possible to achieve the same ends through less intrusive means.

Processing of data collected for monitoring purposes must also comply with the Second Data Protection Principle (specific Purposes) and the requirements for data to be 'adequate, relevant and not excessive' (Third Principle), 'accurate and, where necessary, up to date' (Fourth Principle). The Data Controller should take care to think through what

they are doing, in order to meet all these requirements.

Finally, the personal data must not be held longer
than necessary (Fifth Principle) and must respect
Data Subject rights, including that of Subject Access (Sixth Principle).

# 9. The requirement to have good quality data

It is in no one's interest to have poor quality data, but the Act makes it mandatory to take care. You must ensure that your data is:

- adequate, relevant and not excessive (Third Principle);
- accurate and, where necessary, up to date (Fourth Principle).

This means that you must hold enough data but, importantly, not too much. You should always ask yourself whether you actually need a piece of data in order to carry out the Purpose you are obtaining or holding it for. If you don't but would still like to have the information, the least you should do is to make it clear to the Data Subject that they do not have to provide it. Even then, you must be able to show how the information is relevant. If it isn't you shouldn't be holding it, even if the Data Subject offers it.

Because the data you do hold must be accurate, it is worth thinking from the outset about how you are going to keep it that way. This starts with deciding what information to collect and how to get it. Good design of your data capture forms can help; so can choosing reliable and up to date sources if you are not acquiring the data directly from the Data Subject. Once you have the data, no matter where you acquired it from, it is your responsibility to keep it accurate and up to date. You need to assess how volatile it is likely to be, and therefore how often you may need to verify it. You also need to ensure that your system gets properly updated if you are notified of any changes. And finally, any information that you yourself generate — such as a record of your transactions with the Data Subject — must also be accurately recorded.

# Examples

- In the light of the new Act I decide to review the records I hold on the users of my enquiry service. The first question is whether I need to hold any personal data at all. The enquiries are all dealt with by phone, and most are answered orally. For these, it is not necessary to ask who the person is, although for statistical purposes it would be useful to know what part of the country they are calling from. I might be tempted to use automatic caller line identification (CLI) to discover the phone number they were calling from and record that (which in most cases would tell me their location). On reflection I decide that that would be irrelevant and excessive — and in the case of mobile phones would not give me the information I need, so would be inadequate. In addition I would be collecting information without the Data Subject knowing, so it might well be 'unfair'. I therefore decide instead to ask at the end of the call whether the Data Subject would mind telling me where they are calling from. A few callers are also offered a written information sheet. To send these, I obviously need to ask for their address. However, once I have sent the information I no longer need the full address, so I decide that it would be excessive to put it into the system. Instead, I write the address straight onto the envelope, with a code to indicate which information sheet to enclose.

- I run a youth information service. The information I give has to be tied in very closely to people's ages as their entitlement to different services changes as they get older. I therefore decide that I should ask for and record enquirers' date of birth. This does not go out of date, so is more likely to remain accurate, and I can justify it as being relevant and not excessive. A colleague runs a summer scheme for local children. They only attend for three weeks, and the activities they do are only roughly related to their age. My colleague therefore decides that asking for date of birth might be excessive, and instead asks them to select an age band when they sign up.

- My directory is compiled from a number of sources, some more accurate than others. Because I realise that printed directories are almost bound to be out of date, and particularly because I don't fully trust all the sources, I decide to ask everyone I intend to include to check their own details before publication. This also allows me to inform them of what I am doing and ask for their consent to appearing in the directory.

• My information service is mainly provided to organisations, but we do record the name of the person making each enquiry. We also hold a contact name for annual renewals. After reviewing our policy, we decide that the contact name can be fully justified. If it changes, and the organisation forgets to tell us, this won't matter much. Using the name will still help the renewal notice to reach the right part of the organisation, and each year they will get a new opportunity to correct it. We do, however, decide that we should limit the length of time we hold the names of the people who enquire. A short period can be justified, in case there is a follow-up call or a query about the use they are making of the service. We decide that a year is reasonable for this; after that we will archive basic details of the call, but remove the personal data.

# 10. Archive and destruction policies

The requirement in the Fifth Data Protection Principle not to hold information longer than necessary might appear daunting. Very little guidance is given in the Act as to how to assess what is 'necessary'. The starting point is the Purpose(s). Keeping the information must be necessary for the Purpose(s) it is being held for.

It is up to the Data Controller to make a judgement on what is necessary. The easiest cases are where there are legal or contractual reasons to keep data. For example, detailed financial records may have to be kept for six years. So might records of any advice that was given, in case anyone who had been wrongly advised brought a case against you. The Information Commissioner's draft Code of Practice on personnel records (see the chapter on **Codes of Practice**, page 93) suggests time limits for a variety of employment data, ranging from four months for details of unsuccessful job applicants to 12 years for records relating to accident or injury at work.

Where no guidance is available, a possible approach is to ask yourself two questions:

- Can I envisage a situation in the future when I would be asked for this data?
- Would it matter if I didn't have it?

If the answer to both questions is 'yes', there may be a case for keeping it. If not, you should seriously consider whether it is 'necessary' to keep it any longer. Information which you will often decide to keep includes material that forms part of the history of your organisation — or even, possibly, of the individuals concerned.

A supplementary question is whether you need to keep the personal part of the data. While records of some kind may be necessary, it might be possible to anonymise them or compile the necessary statistics and dispose of the raw data (thus also saving storage space).

Before destroying any data, remember that destruction is a form of 'processing', which must therefore comply with all the Data Protection Principles, including fairness and security (for which see the chapter on **Security**, page 66). It could be unfair to destroy data that someone might reasonably expect to be able to depend on you holding.

# Examples

- My organisation runs conferences. From time to time the information service is asked to compile lists of people working in particular academic areas, so that they can be considered as possible speakers at a forthcoming conference. We build up a small file on each person, with examples of their publications, contact details and so on. This information is not used for anything else, so the question arises of how long we should keep it. We decide that people do not change their area of work or — at this senior level — their place of work very often, and conference topics often come round again. Even if we don't use someone for a particular conference, we may consider them again several years later. So we decide that it would be reasonable, and above all 'fair', to keep the information for about five years. If we have not used it by then there is a higher risk of it being inaccurate or out of date. A colleague in the same situation, however, concludes that this is far too long. It does not take much effort to compile an up to date list of people currently working in a particular area, and it is hard to prove that it is 'necessary' to hold on to information that may well never be used. So in their organisation they compile a new list for each conference as it comes up and destroy it after the decision has been made on whom to invite.

- Our information service sends out free information sheets on a range of topics. Occasionally we announce a new one before it is ready and have to collect the names and addresses of people who ask for a copy. When the information sheet is ready, we send it out to everyone on the list. We decide that we need to keep the list for a week or two, in case anyone doesn't receive it and we need to check whether it was sent, but after that there is no longer any good reason and the list is deleted. We do give people the option of being added to our permanent list, to get future materials on the same topic, but this is something they have to ask for specifically.

- Our database of borrowers has been in existence for twelve years, and contains a complete history of our transactions with each borrower. This is useful for statistics, and we also use the information on overdue books and fine defaults in order to identify people who may be liable to have their access withdrawn. When we review the situation, we realise that for statistical purposes we do not need to be able to identify who has borrowed what; we just need to see the general pattern of borrowing. We therefore arrange that our archive will be anonymised by removing the borrower details. When it comes to the overdue books and fines, we decide that it is excessive and unnecessary to have a complete history for everyone. We draw up a policy on the level of default that should trigger concern, and decide to assess people on an annual basis. We therefore do not need to keep any details of overdue books or fine defaults for most people for longer than a year.

# 11. People's right to see their own records

The right of Subject Access has already existed for over 15 years under the 1984 Data Protection Act, but that only applied to computer records. The 1998 Act now extends this to many manual records as well. While Subject Access rights have been relatively rarely exercised up to now, this could well change once people start to realise that they can see paper records as well. It is as well to be prepared.

The basic position is that when someone makes a valid Subject Access request you have to specify:

- whether any of their personal data is being processed by you, or for you by a Data Processor.
- a description of the data, why you hold it and who it may be disclosed to.
- all *the actual personal data you hold about that Data Subject (but with important exceptions).*
- where you got the information from, if you know.
- the 'logic' involved in any automated decision you make about that Data Subject, unless it is a trade secret.

## The Subject Access procedure

A Subject Access request must be made in writing; it may be sent by electronic means such as fax or e-mail. You cannot insist on people using your own form, but it may be helpful both to you and the Data Subject to have one, as a check that all the information has been provided and conditions complied with. A sample form is shown opposite.

The Data Controller may, but does not have to, charge a fee of up to £10. There is nothing to stop you having a different fee for different circumstances, or different types of Data Subject. A Subject Access request is not valid until you have received any fee due.

You must be careful only to provide the information to the right person. This means that you should ask for information to verify their identity. You may also ask for information to help you locate their records. You might, for example, want to ask what part of your organisation they originally dealt with, or the approximate date they were last in contact. A Subject Access request is not valid until you have received any of this information you need, but you can only ask for 'reasonable' information.

Once you have received a valid Subject Access request you must reply 'promptly' and within a maximum of 40 days.

You do not have to respond if a Subject Access request is made too soon after an identical or similar request from the same Data Subject. In deciding whether it is too soon, you have to consider the type of data, your purpose(s) in holding it, and how often it changes.

When providing access you must explain any codes used, so that the material can be understood by the Data Subject.

# Example subject access form

NAME OF ORGANISATION
Subject Access request (1998 Data Protection Act)

You are entitled to see most of the information we hold about you. If you want to see it, please fill in this form and hand it in to the office, with the required fee.

Your name:

Your address:

A phone number where we can contact you (if you wish):
Please tick if you have ever been:

☐ a user of our information services
☐ a staff member
☐ a trainee on one of our courses

If you have not ticked any of the above, please tell us of any reason why you think we might have information about you:
.........................................................................................................................

If we may have known you under a different name, please tell us that here: ...........................................................................................................

Are you interested in *all* the information we hold, or just part of it?

☐ all the information
☐ just the information about ............................

If we find any information about you, do you want to:

☐ have a look at it at our office
☐ have us send you a copy

I want to see the records you hold on me, as described above, and I enclose £XX.

Signature:

*Please note:*

- If the address you give above does not match the one in our records, or where the information is particularly confidential, we may have to ask you for additional identification.

- We will reply as quickly as we can. We aim to reply within three weeks, but we may take up to 40 days. If you have asked for a copy of the information, we will send it to the address you have given above.

- We have information about people who have used our services, staff, trainees and business contacts. We don't keep this information once we no longer need it, so if you were in touch with us some time ago we may no longer have any information about you.

- We will show you everything we have about you, except that we may be allowed to hold back information which is also about someone else.

# Information you do not have to provide

You do not have to provide a copy of the data if it is not possible to do so or if it would involve disproportionate effort. The Data Subject still has the right to see it, however. The Data Subject may voluntarily limit the extent of the data they wish to see, and may voluntarily view the data without getting a copy, but the choice is theirs not yours.

You are allowed to continue with your normal processing after you have received the request, so that the information eventually released might not be exactly what you held at the time of the request being made. What you must not do is make any changes specifically in order to make the record you release more palatable to the Data Subject, or less embarrassing to you.

Public bodies, and certain voluntary organisations, are able to withhold parts of the data held in specified health, education, social work and housing records if an appropriate authorised person certifies that the Data Subject would be harmed by access. Guidance notes on all these special cases are available from the Information Commissioner.

You do not have to reveal your intentions towards someone you are in negotiation with if access would be likely to prejudice those negotiations. Likewise, you do not have to give access to personal data that is being used for management forecasting or management planning if this would be likely to prejudice the conduct of the business.

You do not have to give access to confidential references which you have *given* in respect of the Data

Subject. If they want to see a reference, they would have to apply to the recipient, who would then have to judge whether to show it or not (which would include asking you whether you consent).

Further exemptions from Subject Access apply, for example, to information which benefits from legal professional privilege, and to some information held by the armed forces or for government and judicial appointments.

Above all, you may be able to withhold part of any record that identifies a third party, either within the data or as the source of the data. The rules are complex, and are described further below.

## When can you withhold third party information?

When you give someone access to the information you hold about them, you *may* be able to withhold parts of the record that relate to other people. However, this is not automatic. Firstly, the third party must be identifiable by the Data Subject (whether or not they are identifiable by you). If someone cannot be identified either from the data or as the source of the data, you must not withhold the information relating to them.

Even if there is an identifiable third party, you then have to try to find out whether or not they agree to the information relating to them being revealed. You cannot assume that they do not agree, unless they have already made this explicit. Even if they don't agree, you have to decide whether they are being reasonable.

If you decide that you have grounds for withholding the material relating to the third party, you still have to show the Data Subject as much as you can, by editing out any identifying details if possible and showing the rest of the information.

This is summarised in the chart below.

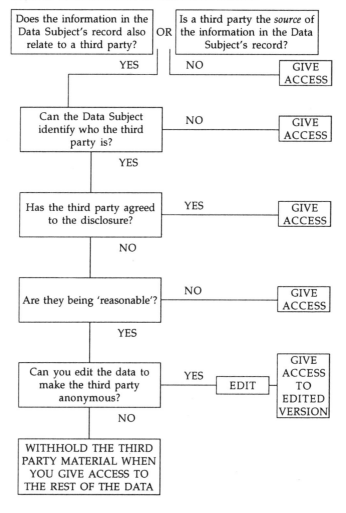

NB: The chart opposite is only to do with Subject Access; it doesn't apply to disclosure to others.

# Examples

- Most of the personnel records in our company are held centrally, but each line manager keeps a small file on each of the people in their department, the contents of which are entirely up to the manager. One day a staff member makes a Subject Access request, and only gets the central record. They complain. We consider arguing that the line manager's file is not a 'relevant filing system', but decide in the end that it would be better to review our policy altogether. Managers are given better guidance on what they may and may not keep in their personnel files, and these files are included in response to Subject Access requests.

- One of our borrowers asks to see their record. We print it off and post it to them. Three days later they are back asking for an explanation of all the codes the computer system has used. We realise that we should produce a standard explanation of all the codes, so that anyone in future can understand what their print-out means.

- My loans system records borrowers' addresses. One day someone comes in with a ticket and asks to make a Subject Access request under that name. They fill in the form, leaving the address blank. When I query this they say that they want to collect the response in person, so I don't need their address. While the request might be genuine, it is also possible that the person in front of me has just found the ticket and is trying to obtain additional information about the holder. I explain that they must provide the address and some other identifying details if they want to view the record or collect a copy in person. Otherwise I would be happy to take their £10 and post the copy to the address we hold.

• A parent asks to make a Subject Access request for their student daughter's borrowing record in our academic library, making it quite clear that they are doing so to check up on how much work she has been doing. While their motives are none of my business, I have to make it clear that only the Data Subject has a right to make a Subject Access request (with some exceptions for children, and in particular their school and health records).

• A member of the public makes a complaint about one of our front-desk staff. It is considered not serious enough to warrant investigation, but the line manager decides that it should be put on the staff member's file in case any further similar complaints are made. (This may not be best practice, but that is not the issue here.) The staff member suspects what has happened and makes a Subject Access request. Do we have to show them the complaint? When we review the file, we find that the complainant has marked their letter 'confidential'. We write to them and ask if they would be happy for the staff member to see the letter. They reply 'no'. We then decide that it would be possible to edit the letter of complaint to make it impossible for the staff member to identify the complainant. This involves making a photocopy and deleting the identifying details — not only the name and contact details of the complainant, but also the date and other specific details of the complaint. This is the version that the staff member has access to.

- See also examples given by the Information Commissioner on tricky situations which may arise with Subject Access. These can be found in the paper on Subject Access and Third Party Information available on the Commissioner's web site under Guidance and other publications: Compliance Advice.

# 12. Restrictions on direct marketing

For the first time in the UK, the Act gives individuals the right to prevent people using their details for direct marketing. Additional regulations place further restrictions on marketing by phone and fax.

## What is direct marketing?

Although the Act does not define direct marketing precisely, guidance from the Information Commissioner suggests that its scope may be considerably wider than one might think.

Certainly the means of communication is immaterial. The Act defines direct marketing as *unsolicited* communication 'by whatever means' directed to an individual. What it does not specify is the content of the communication. At the time of writing, 'direct marketing' should be taken to apply to material relating to:

- anything you are trying to sell, whether goods (such as publications) or services;
- requests for donations of money or, possibly, time to support an organisation or cause;

but not to:

- material directed to a company or organisation (even if you use a contact name to get it to the right part of the organisation);

- advertisements, flyers and inserts which are included with a magazine or mailing, but which are not the main part of the mailing and go automatically to everyone;

- material which is part of an existing relationship (such as notice of your AGM sent to members).

- material the Data Subject has requested, for example in response to an advertisement.

The material must be inviting people to enter into a new transaction with you. This would include you asking previous customers to make a new purchase. It is not marketing, however, to chase up outstanding payments or to follow up an event by asking participants to evaluate it.

Areas which are not clear include, for example:

- Inviting existing subscribers to an information service to renew their subscriptions.

- Invitations to a free event, such as the preview of an art exhibition in your foyer.

## The Data Subject's rights

The Act specifies that the Data Subject can 'require' a Data Controller in writing not to use their details for direct marketing. There is nothing to prevent you acting on an oral request, but you don't have to.

Having received notice from a Data Subject exercising their right, you must ensure that it is applied consistently across all the activities of the Data Controller, not just the department it was addressed to. This will require reliable organisation-wide procedures.

You should also ensure that the Data Subject's details are 'suppressed' from any disclosure to other organisations for direct marketing purposes.

It is not sufficient to 'clean' your lists against voluntary schemes such as the Mailing Preference Service. While this is obviously good practice, you also have to take account of any specific requirements notified by your Data Subjects.

Direct marketing also has to comply with the Data Protection Principles, including specified Purpose(s) (Second Principle). This means that if you are collecting data which will be used, among other things, for direct marketing you must make sure that the Data Subjects know this.

You also need to consider whether it is 'fair' (First Principle) to tell them that you will use their data for direct marketing but without giving them the opportunity there and then to exercise their right to opt out. It would clearly be good practice to have an 'opt-out' box for people to tick if they do not want their details used for direct marketing. It is probably wise to regard this as a requirement. What you certainly must not do is to put unnecessary obstacles in the way of a Data Subject who wants to exercise their rights.

# Direct marketing by phone and fax: the Telecommunications (Data Protection & Privacy) Regulations 1999

Although they are not part of the Data Protection Act, the Telecommunications (Data Protection & Privacy) Regulations 1999 are enforced alongside the Act by the Information Commissioner.

Among other things, these Regulations give individuals the right to restrict tele-marketing calls and give businesses the right to restrict tele-marketing faxes. At the time of writing no equivalent provisions apply to e-mail.

For these purposes it is the telephone or fax *number* that counts. An individual (or a partnership or unincorporated association) may 'notify' a caller not to make any further marketing calls to that number. The telephone subscriber (the person named on the bill) may also place the number on a central register operated by the Telephone Preference Service (TPS). No one may then make marketing calls to that number, regardless of where they acquire the number — the phone book, a bought in list, previous contact with the Data Subject, or even dialling at random. There is no provision for differentiation between different Data Subjects who use the same line; it is the number that is either barred from use or not.

The only exception to this rule is where the subscriber has specifically given the caller permission to make marketing calls, and thus to over-ride any existing or future entry of their number on the TPS register.

Anyone making a marketing call to a number after they have been told not to, or more than 28 days after it has been placed on the TPS register, unless they have obtained permission from the subscriber, is committing an offence. Marketing has essentially the same definition here as it does for the Data Protection Act.

A similar Fax Preference Service (FPS) applies to business lines, while the sending of unsolicited marketing faxes to non-business lines is outlawed entirely unless the subscriber opts in. In practice many tele-marketers find it hard to distinguish between the two types of line, and the FPS does allow non-business lines to be placed on its register.

What this means for anyone intending to carry out marketing by phone or fax is summarised in the chart opposite. For each number you must know whether the call or fax is permitted. This requires you to keep good records of expressed opt-ins or opt-outs as well as checking against the TPS and FPS registers. Checking can be done on an *ad hoc* basis or by subscription to regular updates of the register(s). See **Contacts** on page 105 for further details.

# Can you make that marketing call/ fax?

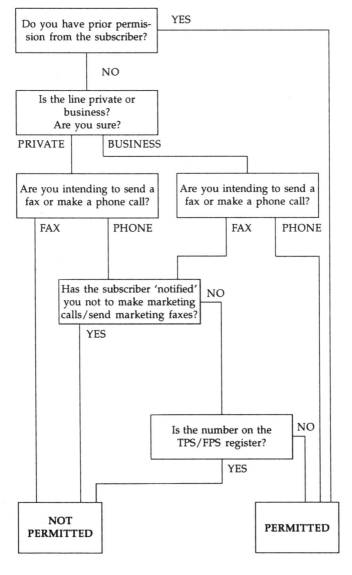

# Examples

- Subscribers to my information service get a renewal notice each year. Because this is just an extension of their existing service, I decide that it does not count as direct marketing, even if I include information with the notice about upgrading from the 'silver' to the 'gold' service. However, a professional association approaches me to use the list of subscribers for material about joining the association. Because the information would clearly be directed at the individuals, not the organisations they work for, I decide that in supplying the list I must omit anyone who has opted out of direct marketing. (I must also, of course, be sure that the use of the data is 'compatible' with the purpose(s) I originally collected it for, and that the Data Subjects know of this possible disclosure.)

- After I have run a training course, I like to keep track of who has participated so that I can invite them to follow-up courses and conferences, or perhaps advertise relevant publications they may want to buy. Because I am directing this marketing to the individuals who have participated on the course, even if they did so on behalf of their employer, I need to take account of their right to opt out. I therefore amend my booking form to explain that I will keep people's details for this purpose, unless they wish to opt out by ticking a box.

# 13.  Other Data Subject rights

In summary, the Data Subject's rights under the Act include:

- To have information about who is using their data and for what (see Chapter 4).

- To withhold consent to the use made of their data in some cases (see Chapter 5).

- To opt out of direct marketing and tele-marketing (see Chapter 12).

- To restrict automated decision-making (see below).

- To prevent processing that causes harm to the Data Subject (see below).

- To apply for Subject Access (see Chapter 11).

- To ask the Data Protection Commissioner to make an 'Assessment' of whether an organisation or person is complying with the Act (see Chapter 20).

## Automated decision-making

Data Subjects have the right to 'require' a Data Controller, in writing, not to make any decisions about them entirely automatically.

If they have not done this, decisions may be made automatically, but they have the right to know 'as soon as reasonably practicable' that this is happening. They then have the right to ask for the decision to be reconsidered manually within 21 days. They can go to court to enforce these rights if the Data Controller does not comply with them.

In brief, these rules do not apply if:

- the automated decision is taken in connection with a legal responsibility or a contract involving the Data Subject, *and*

- the effect of the decision is to grant their request *or* their interests are safeguarded (for example by allowing them to 'make representations').

## Processing that harms the Data Subject

The Data Subject has the right to 'require' the Data Controller, in writing, to stop processing their personal data in ways that harm the Data Subject. Harm is defined as 'substantial damage or substantial distress' that is 'unwarranted'.

This right is only available if the Data Controller is relying on the fifth or sixth fair processing conditions in Schedule 2: the official functions and the 'legitimate interests' of the Data Controller. If the processing is in connection with a contract, for example, the Data Subject cannot prevent it.

If the right is exercised the Data Controller must reply in writing within 21 days, either agreeing to stop or saying why they don't think they should. The Data Subject can take the Data Controller to court if they don't think they have complied properly.

# Legal remedies

Many Data Protection problems will be resolved directly with the Data Controller or through the intervention of the Information Commissioner. For most Data Subjects court action will be a last resort. This section is therefore a very brief summary.

A Data Subject may use the court to enforce other rights within the Act, such as those described immediately above and the right of Subject Access.

Where someone has suffered 'damage' by a contravention of the Act they can take the Data Controller to court for compensation (and may also claim for associated distress).

The court may order the Data Controller to 'rectify, block, erase or destroy' inaccurate data. This applies even if the mistake was made by someone else who provided the data. Alternatively the court may order the Data Controller to add a statement to the record rebutting the inaccuracy. In addition the court may order the Data Controller to notify anyone to whom they have disclosed the inaccurate information, if this is 'reasonably practicable'.

Where the Data Controller is required to make corrections, the court may also order them to pass the corrections on to anyone to whom they have disclosed the incorrect information.

# 14. Security

Security must be seen in the context of wider organisational policies. Many aspects of security will be taken care of by, for example, the IT department or its equivalent. However, high level security provision on its own is not enough; the systems have to work in practice. The Seventh Data Protection Principle makes this clear, by requiring that security measures be 'technical and organisational'. Technical measures are relatively easy to provide: password systems, back-up systems for computers, locks on filing cabinets, and access control either to the building or to key parts of it are all routine.

Beyond that, however, all staff — especially those who deal with personal data regularly — need to be aware of what they are allowed to do, what they are not allowed to do, what security procedures they are expected to follow, and whom to ask if they are in any doubt. There must be policies spelling out what is expected, opportunities for staff to know what those policies are and what procedures are required to implement them, and regular checks on whether the policies and procedures are being followed.

Those who have specific security responsibility should refer to the British Standard on Information Security Management, BS7799, which identifies 10 key 'controls':

- Is there a documented security policy?
- Are responsibilities for security processes clearly allocated?
- Are users given adequate security training?
- Are security incidents always reported?
- Is there a virus checking policy?
- Is there a plan for maintaining business continuity?
- Are legal copyright issues always given due consideration?
- Are important organisational records protected?
- Are personal records processed in accordance with the Data Protection Act?
- Are regular security reviews performed?

The biggest risk to security is almost always your own staff. The damage they do can be deliberate — stealing information about people, such as business contacts they want to use for their own purposes, for example, or trashing the database out of frustration on being demoted. More often it is unthinking or inadvertent — giving information over the telephone to someone who shouldn't have it, leaving confidential files on their kitchen table for a neighbour to see when they are working at home, or chatting in the canteen about a user's borrowing habits where other people can overhear.

Even with external threats, the accepted wisdom is that anyone trying to gain access is more likely to succeed by tricking your staff into giving away vital information than by hacking straight into your computer.

Your first line of defence is therefore to ensure that staff are aware of the possibilities and operate within a culture where information, and especially personal data, is handled carefully and responsibly. To support them, you should take measures that make it as easy as possible for them to do the right thing. At the same time you should not be over-anxious. Security measures must be *appropriate* to the threat, not 100% perfect every time. (Even government security agencies have been known to lose vital information held on laptop computers.)

The kind of things the responsible person at the departmental level should be looking at include:

# Physical security

* Is access to confidential information, especially on paper, physically restricted by controls over who can get into the rooms where it is stored or the storage units themselves?

* Are there systems for signing in and out the keys that give access to important data, or the data itself — especially when it is taken off the premises?

* When personal data is used in public places, is it possible for staff to use it, whether on paper or on screen, without it being seen by unauthorised people?

* If staff take work home, have you made appropriate provision for security?

- Are confidential manual files shredded or securely disposed of?

## System design

- Are appropriate passwords and back-up procedures built into your systems (and used)?

- Are systems designed so that confidential or sensitive data is kept separate from more public data, with an additional layer of security?

- Where staff deal with different users, clients or customers one after the other over the counter, does the system automatically force them to clear one person's details from the screen before attending to the next person?

- If staff leave a screen open and get called away, does it close automatically after an appropriate interval?

- Are systems designed so that reports and statistical outputs which do not need to identify individuals are completely anonymous?

- Do your systems require confirmation before significant material can be deleted?

- Although this is not a security issue, do systems assist staff in inputting data that is adequate, relevant, not excessive, accurate and up to date? And do they make it easy to locate all the relevant data in response to a Subject Access request?

# Procedures

- Is there a recognised procedure for verifying the *bona fides* of anyone calling up over the phone and asking about personal data, even if they claim to be the Data Subject (such as using agreed passwords or calling back on a known number)?

- Similarly, if people come in person do your staff know how to check that they are authorised to have any personal data that is disclosed to them?

- Where you routinely exchange information with other organisations, do you have an agreed protocol covering procedures for authorisation?

- Do your staff clear their working area of personal data before leaving the office (and letting the cleaners in)?

One area that often gives rise to concern is e-mail. Although the dangers can be exaggerated, it is important to be aware that e-mail is inherently insecure. E-mails themselves may constitute personal data if the addressee is identifiable. More importantly, if e-mail is used for sending personal data to other people, some thought should be given as to whether it should be encrypted.

The lists above are not comprehensive. They do not cover many points which would normally be dealt with by the IT department or at an organisation-wide level. An information service or library that was totally responsible for its own security would, for example, have to look in much more detail at back-up procedures, measures against electronic intrusion through viruses or hackers, and steps to prevent loss or unauthorised access through theft or the activities of outside contractors.

# Examples

- I am the team leader in the information department of a medical charity. A new computer system is introduced for holding details of telephone enquiries, which includes a lot of 'sensitive' information. Administrative staff are allowed to access basic contact details, but not the sensitive part; one day, however, one of them goes to the computer and finds that I have been called away urgently, leaving the database open on a very sensitive screen which the administrative worker is normally not able to see. She hasn't been told what to do in this situation, or how to close the screen and get back to her normal view of the data. When I find out, I realise that I shouldn't have left the screen open, even in an emergency. However, it would be better if the system was redesigned to shut down sensitive screens automatically after a set interval of no activity. I also decide that all staff should be given extra training in what to do if they find the system behaving differently from usual.

- Our office contact database contains the home numbers of key-holders and a few other staff, so that they can be contacted in an emergency. One day a relatively new staff

member is on the switchboard, when someone phones up asking for one of these members of staff, who happens not to be in the
office. The caller says that they are a relative,
in town unexpectedly, so the switchboard operator gives them the home number. It later
turns out that the caller is actually an ex-part-
ner who has been harassing our staff member for some time. Disciplinary procedures
are invoked against the operator, for going
against company security policy. However,
she is able to show that her induction procedure didn't cover this policy, and it is therefore the company which is in breach of Data
Protection for not having taken appropriate
organisational security measures.

# 15.  Who can see what?

One of the features of the security requirements in the seventh Data Protection Principle is that precautions must be taken against 'unauthorised' processing. Your staff must therefore not use data in any way that they are not permitted to, and they must not disclose it to anyone else who is not permitted to have it. But in order for this to make sense, someone has to do the authorising. Unless there are clear guidelines on what is permitted, staff cannot be expected to comply.

The second Data Protection Principle says that all processing must be 'compatible' with the purpose(s) it was obtained for. Therefore, in deciding who is authorised to see any particular type of data, it is important to think about what type of access is compatible with the purpose. The personnel department may, for example, hold sensitive data about staff members which it is not appropriate for their line managers, or even the Managing Director to have access to.

In particular, it might be worth asking questions like:

- How much of the information that we hold about these particular Data Subjects needs to be available every time we access their records? Should some of it only be available to staff above a particular level, or carrying out a particular activity?

- If we offer our Data Subjects confidentiality, in what circumstances is it appropriate for their details to be discussed among our staff, so that we can check that we are providing them with the best service?

- Where people who do not normally have access to personal data ask to have it for a specific reason, how much evidence do we need from them to justify handing it over?

- What guidelines do we have for access to personal data by auditors and internal or external quality control monitors? Are there ways they could do their job without seeing the actual personal data?

- In what circumstances will we need to seek consent from the Data Subject before disclosing their data in ways that they have not been pre-warned about?

- What would our reaction be if we were asked by the police, the Department of Social Security or some other official agency for access to personal data?

# Information-sharing agreements

If you are in a situation where you are routinely expecting to share information with other Data Controllers, the arrangements should be put on a formal basis, setting out the types of information to be shared, the purposes, and any mechanisms that will be applied to ensure that the data is handled securely.

If a funding agency, for example, expects you to provide them with personal data about your staff, service users or customers for any reason, this should normally be spelled out in advance in the funding agreement or contract. You can then ensure that your Data Subjects know that this type of disclosure will take place.

## Official requests for access to personal data

The Act does allow you to disclose data in certain circumstances where it would otherwise not be permitted. You are allowed disclose data behind the Data Subject's back, and in ways that are not compatible with the original purpose(s), for example, where the disclosure is for:

- the prevention or detection of crime; or
- the apprehension or prosecution of offenders; or
- the assessment or collection of any tax or duty.

The exemption can be invoked only if applying the normal rules would be 'likely to prejudice' the purpose. The Act does not say that you *must* disclose in these circumstances, merely that if you do, you have not breached the Data Protection Act.

A further exemption from non-disclosure restrictions applies where the law *requires* you to reveal information.

You should, however, be wary of providing personal data to officials just because they ask. They may well have a right to see it, or you may be able to choose to give it, but the Data Protection Act still applies. 'Fishing expeditions' are almost certain not to be permitted. The agency must normally have a good reason for needing the information, and must only ask about specific individuals.

As a minimum it is usually best to get from the requesting agency in writing the legal basis on which they are asking for the information. If it turns out that they were not entitled to have it, this might give you some protection. It will often be appropriate for disclosures in these circumstances to require approval at a high level in your organisation, and perhaps by the legal department.

# 16. Transferring data abroad

The Act implements a European Directive which is intended to provide a framework within which personal data may be transferred freely as long as it is protected. The eighth Data Protection Principle provides that personal data may only be transferred within the European Economic Area (EEA) or to countries which have equivalent protection. At the time of writing Hungary and Switzerland have been assessed by the European Commission as having adequate legislation, with Canada under consideration.

In theory, a Data Controller could make their own judgement as to whether a country provided adequate protection; without specialist knowledge, however, most will prefer to rely on the decisions of the European Commission.

When transferring information outside the UK, the first question is therefore whether the recipient is in a country where adequate Data Protection exists. If so, no special arrangements are necessary. The remainder of this chapter considers cases where the recipient is not in the EEA or in a country on the 'approved list'.

## Conditions under which data may be transferred

Schedule 4 of the Act (see Appendix 4) provides for cases where the eighth Principle may be disregarded. These include, in brief and among other provisions:

- Where the Data Subject has given consent.

- Where the processing is *necessary* in relation to a contract the Data Subject is party to.

- Where the rights and freedoms of the Data Subject are protected in a way approved or authorised by the Information Commissioner.

In many cases, the main way in which it will be possible to comply with the last provision above is through a contract between the Data Controller in the UK and the recipient overseas, a contract whose terms have been approved by the Information Commissioner.

There is another option in the case of transfers to the United States of America, which has been the subject of much negotiation. The US position has been adamantly against introducing legislation which would comply with the EU approach. The compromise eventually arrived at has been the concept of 'safe harbours'. Under this scheme, companies and organisations in the USA can voluntarily sign up to measures to protect personal data and give Data Subjects enforceable rights. Transfer to these 'safe harbours' will then be permitted.

However, the scheme has taken off very slowly, as Data Controllers in the USA are reluctant to undertake the additional responsibilities and incur the associated costs. Successful legal action in early 2001 over the unprotected transfer of personal data from Spain to the USA, however, appears as though it might be a catalyst in promoting greater take-up of the scheme.

Remember that it is not enough *just* to comply with the eighth Data Protection Principle. You have to comply with *all* the Principles, including the 'Fair processing code', the requirement for the disclosure to be 'compatible' with your specified Purpose(s), and the need to have appropriate security against unauthorised access.

# Transfers to specific recipients overseas

If your organisation has a regular relationship with a recipient overseas, arrangements for data transfer can obviously be set up in advance. This would include, for example, regular collaboration with information services, libraries or the like overseas and exchanges of personal data between a parent company and a subsidiary, or between companies in the same group.

The most straightforward case is where the transfer is *necessary* for carrying out or entering into a contract between the Data Subject and the Data Controller, or for a contract that is at the Data Subject's request or in their interests. However, this does not mean that all data you hold about people with whom you have a contract can automatically be transferred. You may only transfer data where it is necessary, and if it would be possible to complete the contract without transferring the data, you may not be able to rely on this provision.

Another straightforward option, in theory, is to obtain consent. Such consent would have to meet the test described in the chapter **When do you need consent?** (see page 22): that it be 'specific, informed and freely given'. This suggests that, at the least, Data Subjects should be told that their data is going to a country where their rights may not be as effectively protected as in the UK. In addition, they must have a genuine right to withhold their consent.

Failing either of these, a contractual arrangement with the recipient (or, in the case of the USA, having the recipient sign up to 'safe harbours') may be required. Because the terms of the contract have to be approved by the Information Commissioner, it is advisable to get detailed information on this from her Office.

One-off or irregular transfers can be approached in the same way, but it may not be worth getting involved in agreeing a contract with the recipient. It will often be easier to get consent from the Data Subject instead.

Further discussion of all these topics can be found in documents available on the Information Commissioner's website (see chapter 23).

## Personal data on your web site

If you put personal data on an open web site, you cannot control who has access to it, or which countries they come from. This means that you are left with very little alternative: you will almost certainly have to have consent from any Data Subject whose details are on your site. (Even just their name and e-mail address is probably enough to count as personal data.)

Slightly different considerations apply when you are *collecting* data on a web site. You still need to make sure that you have complied with all the Data Protection Principles, but there will be more emphasis on ensuring that the Data Subject knows what they are letting themselves in for before they supply their details, through a prominent Data Protection and security statement.

Remember that the Act's definition of a Data Subject makes no distinction about location. Anyone in the world has rights under the Data Protection Act once you obtain their data.

## Examples

- Members of my staff are attending a conference in Russia. Russia is not in the EEA or on the approved list. The contract for places at the conference is between me and the conference organiser, not between me (as Data Controller) and the staff (as Data Subjects). However, it is clearly in their interests, thus meeting the third condition in Schedule 4, so

I do not have to seek consent. However, in order for the processing to be fair, I feel that I should explain to the staff concerned that there may be little I or they can do to control any further use the conference organiser might make of their data.

- A publisher in India asks for the names and addresses of people on my database who might be interested in receiving a new journal. Although there would be a contract if they decide to subscribe, transferring the names for marketing purposes would not be 'at the request of the Data Subject'. I therefore offer my contact in India two options: either I will distribute their publicity for the journal (respecting any marketing opt-outs, of course), or I will approach the individuals concerned to ask for consent to pass their names to India.

- I run an e-mail discussion list in conjunction with a colleague in the USA. Because the names and e-mail addresses of the participants are maintained jointly, they are routinely transferred from me to my colleague and back again. We establish a contract under which my colleague agrees not to use the data for anything else, and to allow any member of the list to exercise their Data Protection rights through me. At the same time we decide that participants in the list should be warned that when they *post* material to the list, their e-mail address will be available to everyone on the list, and may not be fully protected as a result. As long as they only read other participants' postings, their details will not be available.

# 17. Exemptions and other special cases

Very little, if any, personal data is totally exempt from the Act. In specific cases, however, some or all of the Data Protection Principles do not apply. In other cases the Data Subject does not have to be provided with information they may otherwise be entitled to (see also the chapter on **Subject Access**, page 47), or you may be allowed to make a disclosure which would not normally be permitted.

## Research, statistical and historical purposes

There are various exemptions allowing data to be processed for research, which includes statistical and historical purposes, even where this was not the original purpose for its collection. These allow data held for these purposes to be kept indefinitely and to be used regardless of the purpose(s) they were originally obtained for, provided that:

- the processing does not support actions or decisions relating to specific individuals *and*
- the processing does not cause anyone substantial damage or distress.

Personal data which are processed only for research purposes are exempt from Subject Access if they are processed in compliance with the two conditions set out above, and if no Data Subject can be identified in any public results of the research or statistics.

You do not lose the research exemptions merely because the data are disclosed to a researcher or to the Data Subject or someone acting on their behalf (or at their request or with their consent).

# 'Subject information' exemptions

Some of the specific exemptions modify the rules on **'subject information'**. If such an exemption applies:

* You do not have to tell the Data Subject that you are processing their data.
* The Data Subject does not have the right of Subject Access.

As well as the specific restrictions on Subject Access to some social work, health and education records (see the chapter on **Subject Access**, page 47), these may also be exempt from the 'subject information provisions' in certain circumstances.

# 'Non-disclosure' exemptions

Other exemptions modify the normal restrictions on **'non-disclosure'**. If such an exemption applies you can make a *disclosure* of the data, even if it would conflict with some of the Data Protection Principles. The ones you are allowed to break in making the disclosure are:

* the part of the first Data Protection Principle which says that all processing must be fair

(but you must still meet at least one of the conditions for fair processing and the conditions for sensitive data, if applicable)

- the Principles that say you must only use the data for the specified purpose, and that it has to be adequate, relevant, not excessive, accurate, up to date and not held longer than necessary.

For most organisations the main area of interest is likely to be the exemption from the 'non-disclosure provisions' in *any case* where the disclosure is for one of the 'crime and taxation' purposes. See the chapter on **Who can see what?**, page 73 for further discussion of this.

## Freedom of expression

There is a 'freedom of expression' exemption from all the Data Protection Principles except the seventh Principle (Security) for genuine journalistic, artistic and literary purposes. The Act specifies the conditions which have to be met for this to apply. These include that the processing must be for publication and in the public interest.

If your organisation is involved in publishing or other relevant activities, further details of this exemption may be worth pursuing.

## Domestic use

Personal data processed *by an individual* only for their 'personal, family or household affairs (including recreational purposes)' is exempt from:

- All the Data Protection Principles.
- Subject Access and other individual rights.
- Notification.

Even where the exemption applies, the Data Protection Commissioner still has enforcement powers; in other words she could still issue an Information Notice to check on what you were doing.

# National security

There are wide-ranging exemptions that apply to national security, including exemption from all the Data Protection Principles.

# Transition period for old manual files

In respect of personal data held on computer, and your current paper files, the Act is fully in force from 24 October 2001.

However, there is a limited transition period until 23 October 2007 for old manual files. The transitional provisions only apply to manual material which was already *in your possession* on 24 October 1998.

During the transition period, eligible material does not have to comply with:

- the provisions under the first Data Protection Principle for the Data Subject to know who is processing their data and what for;
- the second Principle (specified purposes);

- the third Principle (adequate, relevant and not excessive);

- the fourth Principle (accurate and up to date);

- the fifth Principle (not held longer than necessary);

- the part of the Act that allows them to go to court to have inaccurate data corrected.

However, Data Subjects do have Subject Access to these old manual files.

# 18. Notification

The focus of the 1984 Act was registration. Once a Data User (the equivalent of a Data Controller) had registered their data processing activities with the Data Protection Registrar (now the Information Commissioner), they were then permitted to carry out those activities. The old Data Protection Principles did not contain the requirement for the Data Subject to know what was going on, and the Data Subject had very few rights to restrict the Data Controller's use of their data.

Under the 1998 Act, the emphasis is reversed. Registration still exists — now termed 'notification' — but the main emphasis is on the responsibilities of the Data Controller and the rights of the Data Subject.

Most Data Controllers still have to notify, although some activities are exempt from notification. These include:

* all manual processing;
* computer-based processing for 'core business purposes'.

Core business purposes are explained in detail in a self-assessment guide available from the Information Commissioner. They are, in brief:

- personnel administration, including payroll and pensions;
- accounts and customer and supplier records;
- marketing, promotion and public relations;
- membership records of non-profit organisations.

Notification costs £35 a year and is renewable annually. In general a Data Controller may make only one notification, covering all the activities they have to notify (plus any that are exempt from notification that they choose to notify voluntarily).

This means that anyone running an information service or library will only have responsibility for notification if they are the Data Protection Compliance Officer for their organisation. Otherwise, they will have to provide information about their activities to whoever is making the notification.

Notification requires the Data Controller to identify the Purposes for which they process personal data, and then for each Purpose the types of Data Subject, types of Data and types of potential disclosure, plus any transfers outside the EEA.

Purposes defined by the Information Commissioner which may be particularly applicable to library and information activities include:

- Staff administration.
- Accounts and records.
- Advertising, marketing and public relations.
- Administration of membership records.
- Consultancy and advisory services.

- Education.
- Information and databank administration.
- Research.
- Trading/sharing in personal information.

The full list, with additional explanation and descriptions, is in the Information Commissioner's publication *Notification Handbook: a complete guide to notification.*

# Notification procedure

For those who do have the responsibility, notification can be initiated in two ways:

- by phone, to the Data Protection Commissioner. At the time of writing the number is 01625 545740
- on the internet. At the time of writing the web address is www.dpr.gov.uk

In either case you first have to provide details of the Data Controller. Guidance is available from the Information Commissioner on how to complete these details. For example, in the case of a limited company you have to provide the full company name, not a trading name.

In an attempt to simplify the notification process, once you have indicated the general nature of your activities the Information Commissioner will produce a draft notification based on 'typical' activities for that type of business. This will be sent to you (if you phoned up), or can be printed off (if you used the internet). You make any corrections necessary, sign it, and send it off with the fee.

You may also find that a model notification entry has been prepared by a professional body or industry consortium and accepted by the Commissioner. If a suitable model exists, this will save considerable time. At the time of writing, the Information Commissioner's web site offers templates, for example, for various types of local authority and educational establishment, but not specifically for libraries or information services.

If the model you use or the draft you receive from the Commissioner doesn't accurately reflect what you do, you can add or delete Purposes and within each Purpose, Data Subjects, Data Classes, recipients and overseas transfers. In each case you can make up your own entry if the standard ones really don't apply. You cannot normally use a Purpose twice.

One feature from the 1984 registration scheme which is missing from notification is the need to indicate your sources of information. In addition the standard lists of potential Data Subjects, Data Classes and recipients are significantly shorter. It should therefore be easier to decide whether or not they apply, making completion of the forms both quicker and more accurate.

In the final part of the notification you have to describe in general terms your security measures, together with various other pieces of additional information.

Once your notification has been accepted it remains valid for one year. Near the end of that time the Commissioner will remind you to renew it.

You have to keep your notification up to date. So if any of the details change, either about the Data Controller or about your activities, you have to ensure that an amendment form is submitted within 28 days. There is no charge for this. Failure to do it is a criminal offence.

You cannot transfer a notification. This means that if you change your legal status (for example amalgamating with another organisation) the new organisation has to notify from scratch in its own right.

# 19. Codes of practice

An important new provision in the 1998 Act is that the Information Commissioner now has both a power and a duty to promote good practice. In particular she can endorse Codes of Practice for particular types of activity or industry sectors. If she believes a Code of Practice is necessary and the industry has not produced one, she can even impose one of her own.

At the time of writing, no Codes of Practice with particular relevance to library or information services have been published. These would, however, be a welcome development, and it is very likely that industry bodies or other national interest groups will produce relevant Codes of Practice in future.

It will not be a legal requirement to follow a recognised Code of Practice but the Codes will, on the one hand, provide a useful framework for an organisation drawing up its own policies and, on the other, provide a yardstick for anyone making judgements about an organisation's Data Protection practice.

## Personnel Code of Practice

Meanwhile, a draft Code of Practice has been produced covering the use of personal data in the employer/employee relationship. It is worth taking a look at this, to see what the Information Commissioner has in mind for Codes of Practice.

At the same time, it is important to note that there has been significant opposition to parts of the draft Code. The Information Commissioner has, understandably, tried to indicate the practice which she feels would be in the best interests of the Data Subject. Employers' bodies have argued that the draft Code imposes unrealistic burdens and expectations on the Data Controller. While the Code was originally expected to be finalised in early 2001, this date was pushed back when the extent of opposition became clear.

The draft Code makes clear which provisions are mandatory and which the Information Commissioner feels constitute best practice. However, there is scope for argument over the interpretation of even the mandatory requirements. For example, there has been much debate about the proposed guidance on employee monitoring.

What can safely be said is that anyone who feels able to comply with the draft Code will almost certainly be well compliant with the Code which is finally adopted.

# 20. Enforcement and penalties

The Data Protection Act is enforced by the Information Commissioner, currently Elizabeth France. The Commissioner also enforces the Telecommunications (Data Protection & Privacy) Regulations 1999. The Commissioner's Office is an independent regulatory authority, reporting directly to parliament.

The Commissioner does not have a large staff, and is funded by income from notification fees and other charges, not by government grant.

The 1998 Act has considerably strengthened the enforcement powers of the Commissioner, and her staff for the first time have powers of entry and inspection when they are investigating breaches of the Act.

## Notification

Notification is one aspect of enforcement. Processing without having notified when you should have done so is an offence. This is a 'strict liability' offence: you cannot argue that you did your best. It is also an offence not to keep your notification up to date. On this you *can* argue that you exercised 'due diligence'.

## Assessments

Anyone may ask the Information Commissioner to make an Assessment as to whether a Data Controller appears to be complying with the Act. The person making the request must believe themselves to be directly affected by the processing they want assessed. The Commissioner *must* then make an assessment, provided she has enough information to identify the person making the request and the processing in question.

The Commissioner can choose how to make the Assessment. She can specifically take into account:

- Whether the request raises a matter of substance.
- Any undue delay in making the request.
- Whether the person is entitled to make a Subject Access request.

What this appears to mean is that requests for Assessment should not be used when the matter could have been resolved directly with the Data Controller or through a Subject Access request. If the Commissioner thinks this is the case, it may affect how the Assessment is carried out.

The Commissioner has to tell the person making the request whether she has made an Assessment, and may — but is not obliged to — tell them the outcome.

An Assessment is only the Commissioner's opinion, but would obviously carry some weight if the matter later came to court.

# Information notices

The Commissioner may issue a Data Controller with an Information Notice, either as part of an Assessment or for reasons of·her own. This will ask the Data Controller to provide specific information within a specified time limit, with the aim of enabling the Commissioner to decide whether the Data Protection Principles are being complied with.

Failure to comply with an Information Notice is an offence, unless the Data Controller can show that they 'exercised due diligence' to comply. The Data Controller can appeal against an Information Notice to the Data Protection Tribunal.

# Enforcement notices

Where the Commissioner is satisfied that the Act has been contravened she can issue an Enforcement Notice, telling the Data Controller what they must do in order to bring their activities into line.

Failure to comply with an Enforcement Notice is an offence, unless the Data Controller can show that they 'exercised due diligence' to comply. The Data Controller can appeal against an Enforcement Notice to the Data Protection Tribunal.

# Powers of entry

The Commissioner can apply for a warrant from a circuit judge to enter and inspect premises if she has reasonable grounds for suspecting that an offence under the Act has been committed or the Data Protection Principles are being broken.

The warrant may only be granted if the Data Protection Commissioner has tried to get access by agreement and been refused, unless the judge is convinced that giving advance warning would defeat the object.

It is a criminal offence to obstruct a warrant, with a maximum fine of £5,000.

## Individual offences

In addition to the offence of obstructing a warrant, individuals commit an offence if they 'knowingly or recklessly' obtain or disclose personal data without consent from the Data Controller. Possible defences include having the 'reasonable belief' that what they did was permissible.

If a person has obtained data they are not entitled to, it is a further offence to sell it or offer to sell it.

## Penalties

All offences under the Act, except obstructing a warrant, can be tried either in the Magistrate's Court or the Crown Court. The maximum penalty is a fine of £5,000 in the Magistrate's Court or an unlimited fine in the Crown Court.

Who gets taken to court, should it come to that, depends on the offence. Where the offence is an individual one, it is obviously the individual who would be charged. Where the organisation has committed an offence to do with notification or not cooperating with the Commissioner, the organisation would be charged. The directors or senior officers of a company may also be *personally liable* if they consented to or connived at the offence, or if they were negligent.

# 21. The Data Protection Compliance Officer

It will be clear from the discussion elsewhere in this book that good Data Protection is not just a matter of having a paper policy; it depends very much on what happens day to day. It is therefore important not just to rely on the perhaps remote expertise of an organisation's central Data Protection Compliance Officer, or indeed someone external to the organisation.

The role of a central officer or body is likely to include:

- setting out general organisational policies, linking Data Protection with confidentiality and security where relevant;
- ensuring consistency in the processing of similar data across the organisation (for example personnel records);
- the Notification process;
- handling Subject Access requests;
- providing advice to other parts of the organisation when Data Protection issues arise that are outside their experience.

Within a library or information service the person with Data Protection responsibility, should expect to be responsible for:

- drawing up detailed departmental policies and procedures;
- briefing or training staff;
- acting as an immediate reference point for out-of-the-ordinary situations;
- liaising with the central Compliance Officer over Notification and any major issues.

Of these, it can be argued that briefing or training staff who deal with personal data is the most important. What makes the biggest difference is the actions that they take, day to day, when faced with a decision that has Data Protection implications. In particular they should be aware of their responsibilities in the area of security, and the potential problems that might arise from unauthorised access to personal data.

It may be worth making staff aware, not just of organisational policies, but also of their potential personal liability if they fail to take adequate care.

# 22. References and further reading

Much guidance on the Data Protection Act is available from the Information Commissioner (see **Contacts** below).

Books on Data Protection include:

- Carey, P. *Blackstone's Guide to the Data Protection Act 1998*, Blackstone.

- Ticher, P. *Data Protection for Voluntary Organisations*, Directory of Social Change, 2000.

- Mullock, J. and Leigh-Pollitt, P. *The Data Protection Act 1998 Explained*, Stationery Office Points of Law series, 2000.

- Jay, R. and Hamilton, A. *Data Protection: Law and Practice*, 1999.

- Rayner, C. *Data Protection in the Education Sector, A guide for good practice*, 1999.

The relevant legislation on topics covered in this book includes:

- The Data Protection Act 1998 (1998 Chapter 29)
- The Regulation of Investigatory Powers Act 2000 (2000 Chapter 23)

Acts of Parliament are available from HMSO and at www.hmso.gov.uk/acts.htm

- The Data Protection (Conditions under Paragraph 3 of Part II of Schedule 1) Order 2000 (SI 2000 No. 185)

- The Data Protection (Notification and Notification Fees) Regulations 2000 (SI 2000 No. 188)

- The Data Protection (Subject Access) (Fees and Miscellaneous Provisions) Regulations 2000 (SI 2000 No. 191)

- The Data Protection (Subject Access Modification) (Health) Order 2000 (SI 2000 No. 413)

- The Data Protection (Subject Access Modification) (Education) Order 2000 (SI 2000 No. 414)

- The Data Protection (Subject Access Modification) (Social Work) Order 2000 (SI 2000 No. 415)

- The Data Protection (Processing of Sensitive Personal Data) Order 2000 (SI 2000 No. 417)

- The Data Protection (Designated Codes of Practice) (No. 2) Order 2000 (SI 2000 No. 1864)

- The Telecommunications (Lawful Business Practice) (Interception of Communications) Regulations 2000 (SI 2000 No. 2699)

- The Telecommunications (Data Protection and Privacy) Regulations 1999 (SI 1999 No. 2093)

- The Telecommunications (Data Protection and Privacy) (Amendment) Regulations 2000 (SI 2000 No. 157)

Statutory Instruments can be obtained from The Stationery Office and at www.hmso.gov.uk/stat.htm

# 23. Contacts

It is the Information Commissioner's intention to produce written guidance on various aspects of the Act, in response both to demand from enquirers and to her own priorities. This guidance is normally free. The most useful source of further information is therefore the Commissioner. Examples of related activities in other countries can be found in Chapter 16.

**Information Commissioner (previously known as the Data Protection Commissioner)**

Wycliffe House, Water Lane, Wilmslow, Cheshire SK9 5AF

| | |
|---|---|
| Switchboard: | 01625 545700 |
| Fax: | 01625 545510 |
| Information: | 01625 545745 |
| | www.dataprotection.gov.uk (this website also shows contacts in other countries) |
| | mail@dataprotection.gov.uk |
| Notification: | 01625 545740 |
| | www.dpr.gov.uk |
| | mail@notification.demon.co.uk |

## Telephone Preference Service

This is run by the Direct Marketing Association, under contract to the Department of Trade and Industry. An information pack for tele-marketers who want to know more is available from the TPS.

5th floor, Haymarket House, 1 Oxendon Street, London SW1Y 4EE

| | |
|---|---|
| Tel: | 020 7766 4420 |
| Fax: | 020 7976 1886 |
| e-mail: | tps@dma.org.uk |

To register a phone line not to receive unsolicited marketing: 0845 070 0707

To register a business fax line not to receive unsolicited marketing: 0845 070 0702

## Home Office

The Government Department with Data Protection responsibility is the Home Office. Some useful material can be found on their web site at: www.homeoffice.gov.uk/foi/datprot.htm (*sic*)

## Legal advice

Legal firms specialising in this field will be listed in various directories, although perhaps under broad headings such as Intellectual Property. It would also be worth checking with national profession law associations as to whether they maintain such lists.

# 24. Appendices

[Reproduced from the Data Protection Act 1998 (Ch. 29). Crown Copyright 1998]

## Appendix 1: The Data Protection Principles

1. Personal data shall be processed fairly and lawfully and, in particular, shall not be processed unless-

   (a) at least one of the conditions in Schedule 2 is met, and

   (b) in the case of sensitive personal data, at least one of the conditions in Schedule 3 is also met.

2. Personal data shall be obtained only for one or more specified and lawful purposes, and shall not be further processed in any manner incompatible with that purpose or those purposes.

3. Personal data shall be adequate, relevant and not excessive in relation to the purpose or purposes for which they are processed.

4. Personal data shall be accurate and, where necessary, kept up to date.

5. Personal data processed for any purpose or purposes shall not be kept for longer than is necessary for that purpose or those purposes.

6.  Personal data shall be processed in accordance with the rights of data subjects under this Act.

7.  Appropriate technical and organisational measures shall be taken against unauthorised or unlawful processing of personal data and against accidental loss or destruction of, or damage to, personal data.

8.  Personal data shall not be transferred to a country or territory outside the European Economic Area unless that country or territory ensures an adequate level of protection for the rights and freedoms of data subjects in relation to the processing of personal data.

# Appendix 2: Schedule 2, Conditions relevant for purposes of the first principle: processing of any personal data

1.  The data subject has given his consent to the processing.

2.  The processing is necessary-

    (a) for the performance of a contract to which the data subject is a party, or

    (b) for the taking of steps at the request of the data subject with a view to entering into a contract.

3.  The processing is necessary for compliance with any legal obligation to which the data controller is subject, other than an obligation imposed by contract.

4.  The processing is necessary in order to protect the vital interests of the data subject.

5.  The processing is necessary-

    (a) for the administration of justice,

    (b) for the exercise of any functions conferred on any person by or under any enactment,

    (c) for the exercise of any functions of the Crown, a Minister of the Crown or a government department, or

    (d) for the exercise of any other functions of a public nature exercised in the public interest by any person.

6.    (1) The processing is necessary for the pur-
         poses of legitimate interests pursued by the
         data controller or by the third party or par-
         ties to whom the data are disclosed, ex-
         cept where the processing is unwarranted
         in any particular case by reason of preju-
         dice to the rights and freedoms or legiti-
         mate interests of the data subject.

      (2) The Secretary of State may by order
         specify particular circumstances in which
         this condition is, or is not, to be taken to
         be satisfied.

# Appendix 3: Schedule 3, Conditions relevant for purposes of the first principle: processing of sensitive personal data

1.  The data subject has given his explicit consent to the processing of the personal data.

2.  (1) The processing is necessary for the purposes of exercising or performing any right or obligation which is conferred or imposed by law on the data controller in connection with employment.

    (2) The Secretary of State may by order-

    (a) exclude the application of sub-paragraph (1) in such cases as may be specified, or

    (b) provide that, in such cases as may be specified, the condition in sub-paragraph (1) is not to be regarded as satisfied unless such further conditions as may be specified in the order are also satisfied.

3.  The processing is necessary-

    (a) in order to protect the vital interests of the data subject or another person, in a case where-

    (i) consent cannot be given by or on behalf of the data subject, or

    (ii) the data controller cannot reasonably be expected to obtain the consent of the data subject, or

      (b) in order to protect the vital interests of another person, in a case where consent by or on behalf of the data subject has been unreasonably withheld.

4.     The processing-

      (a) is carried out in the course of its legitimate activities by any body or association which-

         (i) is not established or conducted for profit, and

         (ii) exists for political, philosophical, religious or trade-union purposes,

      (b) is carried out with appropriate safeguards for the rights and freedoms of data subjects,

      (c) relates only to individuals who either are members of the body or association or have regular contact with it in connection with its purposes, and

      (d) does not involve disclosure of the personal data to a third party without the consent of the data subject.

5.     The information contained in the personal data has been made public as a result of steps deliberately taken by the data subject.

6.     The processing-

      (a) is necessary for the purpose of, or in connection with, any legal proceedings (including prospective legal proceedings),

      (b) is necessary for the purpose of obtaining legal advice, or

(c) is otherwise necessary for the purposes of establishing, exercising or defending legal rights.

7.  (1) The processing is necessary-

(a) for the administration of justice,

(b) for the exercise of any functions conferred on any person by or under an enactment, or

(c) for the exercise of any functions of the Crown, a Minister of the Crown or a government department.

(2) The Secretary of State may by order-

(a) exclude the application of sub-paragraph (1) in such cases as may be specified, or

(b) provide that, in such cases as may be specified, the condition in sub-paragraph (1) is not to be regarded as satisfied unless such further conditions as may be specified in the order are also satisfied.

8.  (1) The processing is necessary for medical purposes and is undertaken by-

(a) a health professional, or

(b) a person who in the circumstances owes a duty of confidentiality which is equivalent to that which would arise if that person were a health professional.

(2) In this paragraph "medical purposes" includes the purposes of preventative medicine, medical diagnosis, medical research, the provision of care and treatment and the management of healthcare services.

9.　　(1)　The processing-

(a) is of sensitive personal data consisting of information as to racial or ethnic origin,

(b) is necessary for the purpose of identifying or keeping under review the existence or absence of equality of opportunity or treatment between persons of different racial or ethnic origins, with a view to enabling such equality to be promoted or maintained, and

(c) is carried out with appropriate safeguards for the rights and freedoms of data subjects.

(2) The Secretary of State may by order specify circumstances in which processing falling within sub-paragraph (1)(a) and (b) is, or is not, to be taken for the purposes of sub-paragraph (1)(c) to be carried out with appropriate safeguards for the rights and freedoms of data subjects.

10.　　The personal data are processed in circumstances specified in an order made by the Secretary of State for the purposes of this paragraph.

[Under Condition 10, provision has been made, among others, for processing without consent of:

•　　equalities monitoring on criteria of disability or religion, provided the information is not used for making any decisions about individuals.

- confidential counselling, advice, support or care services, where this is in the substantial public interest, and where consent cannot reasonably be obtained or where seeking consent would jeopardise the service.]

# Appendix 4: Schedule 4, Cases where the eighth Principle does not apply

1.  The data subject has given his consent to the transfer.

2.  The transfer is necessary-

    (a) for the performance of a contract between the data subject and the data controller, or

    (b) for the taking of steps at the request of the data subject with a view to his entering into a contract with the data controller.

3.  The transfer is necessary-

    (a) for the conclusion of a contract between the data controller and a person other than the data subject which-

    (i) is entered into at the request of the data subject, or

    (ii) is in the interests of the data subject, or

    (b) for the performance of such a contract.

4.  (1) The transfer is necessary for reasons of substantial public interest.

    (2) The Secretary of State may by order specify-

    (a) circumstances in which a transfer is to be taken for the purposes of sub-paragraph (1) to be necessary for reasons of substantial public interest, and

(b) circumstances in which a transfer which is not required by or under an enactment is not to be taken for the purpose of sub-paragraph (1) to be necessary for reasons of substantial public interest.

5.  The transfer-

(a) is necessary for the purpose of, or in connection with, any legal proceedings (including prospective legal proceedings),

(b) is necessary for the purpose of obtaining legal advice, or

(c) is otherwise necessary for the purposes of establishing, exercising or defending legal rights.

6.  The transfer is necessary in order to protect the vital interests of the data subject.

7.  The transfer is of part of the personal data on a public register and any conditions subject to which the register is open to inspection are complied with by any person to whom the data are or may be disclosed after the transfer.

8.  The transfer is made on terms which are of a kind approved by the Commissioner as ensuring adequate safeguards for the rights and freedoms of data subjects.

9.  The transfer has been authorised by the Commissioner as being made in such a manner as to ensure adequate safeguards for the rights and freedoms of data subjects.

# Appendix 5: Definitions quoted from the Act

## Data

means information which:

(a) is being processed by means of equipment operating automatically in response to instructions given for that purpose,

(b) is recorded with the intention that it should be processed by means of such equipment,

(c) is recorded as part of a relevant filing system or with the intention that it should form part of a relevant filing system, or

(d) does not fall within paragraph (a), (b) or (c) but forms part of an accessible record as defined by section 68;

[Note: an "accessible record" relates to certain health, education, social work and housing records held by public bodies.]

## Data controller

means, subject to subsection (4), a person who (either alone or jointly or in common with other persons) determines the purposes for which and the manner in which any personal data are, or are to be, processed.

## Data processor

means any person (other than an employee of the data controller) who processes data on behalf of the data controller.

**Data subject**

> means an individual who is the subject of personal data.

**Personal data**

> means data which relate to a living individual who can be identified:
>
> (a) from those data, or
>
> (b) from those data and other information which is in the possession of, or is likely to come into the possession of, the data controller,
>
> and includes any expression of opinion about the individual and any indication of the intentions of the data controller or any other person in respect of the individual.

**Processing**

> in relation to information or data, means obtaining, recording or holding the information or data or carrying out any operation or set of operations on the information or data, including-
>
> (a) organisation, adaptation or alteration of the information or data,
>
> (b) retrieval, consultation or use of the information or data,
>
> (c) disclosure of the information or data by transmission, dissemination or otherwise making available, or
>
> (d) alignment, combination, blocking, erasure or destruction of the information or data.

## Relevant filing system

means any set of information relating to individuals to the extent that, although the information is not processed by means of equipment operating automatically in response to instructions given for that purpose, the set is structured, either by reference to individuals or by reference to criteria relating to individuals, in such a way that specific information relating to a particular individual is readily accessible.

## Sensitive personal data

means personal data consisting of information as to-

(a) the racial or ethnic origin of the data subject,

(b) his political opinions,

(c) his religious beliefs or other beliefs of a similar nature,

(d) whether he is a member of a trade union (within the meaning of the Trade Union and Labour Relations (Consolidation) Act 1992),

(e) his physical or mental health or condition,

(f) his sexual life,

(g) the commission or alleged commission by him of any offence, or

(h) any proceedings for any offence committed or alleged to have been committed by him, the disposal of such proceedings or the sentence of any court in such proceedings.

# Index

After a page number, '*bib*' indicates a bibliographical reference, and '*def*' a definition.

Apart from proper names, other terms with initial capitals (e.g. Assessments; Data Controller), as used in the text, have a specific legal meaning within the Data Protection Act.

court records *see* sensitive personal data

covert monitoring 37

crime prevention and detection purposes 85

criminal records *see* sensitive personal data

current awareness service 27

'damage', Data Subject's rights 65

data 3*def*, 6*def*, 118*def*

   *see also* personal data

Data Controller 3*def*, 118*def*

   archive and destruction policies 43

   responsibility

      for Notification 88-89

      overall 10-11, 13, 14

Data Processor 3*def*, 13-14, 118*def*

Data Protection Act (1998) 102*bib*

   Data Protection Principles 8-9, 107-108

   definitions quoted from the Act 118-120

   Schedule 2 ... processing of any personal data 109-110

   Schedule 3 ... processing of sensitive personal data 111-115

   Schedule 4, Cases where the eighth Principle does not apply 116-117

Data Protection Commissioner *see* Information Commissioner

Data Protection Compliance Officer 11-13, 89, 100-101

Data Protection Principles 8-9, 107-108

# Aslib Know How Guides

*Assessing Information Needs: Tools, Techniques and Concepts for the Internet Age (2nd ed)*

*Copyright for Library and Information Service Professionals (2nd ed)*

*Developing a Records Management Programme*

*Disaster Planning for Library and Information Services*

*Effective Financial Planning for Library and Information Services*

*Email for Library and Information Professionals (2nd ed)*

*Evaluation of Library and Information Services (2nd ed)*

*How to Market Your Library Service Effectively (2nd ed)*

*How to Promote Your Web Site Effectively*

*Information Resources Selection*

*The Internet for Library and Information Service Professionals (3rd ed)*

*Intranets and Push Technology: Creating an Information-Sharing Environment*

*Job Descriptions for the Information Profession*

*Knowledge Management: Linchpin of Change*

*Legal Information – What It Is and Where to Find It (2nd ed)*

*Legal Liability for Information Provision*

*Making a Charge for Library and Information Services*

*Managing Change in Libraries and Information Services*

*Managing Film and Video Collections*

*Managing Library Automation*

*Moving Your Library*

*Performance Measurement in Library and Information Services*